To Reggie:

Be a bold witness

Rev. Charles Blackhear

Pro. 4:23

"GO YE...!"

A Command,
Not an Option

Extreme Measures Igniting You into the
Soul Winner You've Longed to Be

CHARLES C. BLACKSHEAR

WestBow
PRESS
A DIVISION OF THOMAS NELSON

WestBow Press books may be ordered through booksellers or by contacting:
WestBow Press
A Division of Thomas Nelson
1663 Liberty Drive
Bloomington, IN 47403
www.westbowpress.com
1-(866) 928-1240

ISBN: 978-1-4497-8668-7 (sc)
ISBN: 978-1-4497-8667-0 (e)
ISBN: 978-1-4497-8669-4 (hc)

Library of Congress Control Number: 2013903639

Printed in the United States of America

WestBow Press rev. date: 04/05/2013

Contents

About the Author

Evangelist Charles C. Blackshear received Jesus Christ as his Lord and Savior at the early age of sixteen in the summer of 1977. He assisted in an after-school Bible study known as the PTL Club, founded at Southwest High School by Bishop Dale C. Bronner. After receiving a prophetic, life-changing word of the Lord from Prophet Brian Mosley, Charles immediately began preaching the gospel with holy boldness because of the unquenchable fire and desire that was in his heart.

In 1979 Charles attended Georgia State University after graduating from Southwest High School in Atlanta, Georgia, the same year. At Georgia State, Charles started an evangelistic ministry known as Outreach for Christ. Many souls were saved, healed, delivered, and received the Holy Spirit baptism as a result of this ministry. After attending Georgia State University, he felt the need to further his spiritual growth, so in 1981 he enrolled in East Texas Bible College in Tyler, Texas, operated by his mentor Rev. R. W. Schambach, who greatly influenced him. After completing his studies, Charles was fueled with righteous indignation to snatch souls from the kingdom of darkness back into the kingdom of light.

In 1984, Evangelist Blackshear met Ms. Betty Waters at a church service where he ministered. Exactly one year later, Betty became his companion, soul mate, and wife. Together, they have become an inseparable team and have a commission from the Lord to spread the gospel of Jesus Christ to the masses all across the world.

His ministry has also been impacted greatly by Evangelist Mario Murillo, who groomed him to a deeper level of massive soul winning through teaching known as Mainstream School of Mass Miracle Soul Winning held in San Francisco. Charles and Betty have attended two consecutive years of these power-packed teachings held by Evangelist Murillo.

No one has influenced him more powerfully than his pastor, mentor, confidant, and spiritual father, Bishop Dale C. Bronner, founder and pastor of Word of Faith Family Worship Cathedral in Austell, Georgia. Bishop Bronner's living example of Christ, which has been exemplified in his life since early high school days, motivated and sparked a zeal blazed with glory in Charles' life.

Since those early days, Evangelist Blackshear has been spreading the gospel across this country and in foreign countries such as Pakistan, India, Africa, Bahamas, Jamaica, Haiti, Alaska, and multiple cities across this great nation.

Evangelist Blackshear has served as keynote speaker in several college programs as well as high school assembly programs. Locally, he has taken the gospel to the streets, universities, homeless shelters, and prisons for over thirty-six years. Evangelist Blackshear is currently the pastor of evangelism at Word of Faith Family Worship Cathedral's Corporate Evangelistic Outreach ministry, known as CEO, and teaches biweekly Foundations in Christianity and Foundations in Priesthood classes. He is also the president and founder of **Restoration of Power Ministries Inc**. This nonprofit evangelistic ministry helps restore the power of God to the body of Christ by igniting churches to better equip themselves for the massive soul-winning harvest. Please visit his web site: www.rpm23.org.

Foreword

By

Bishop Dale C. Bronner, D. Min.

The Bible teaches the principle that the last shall be first, and the first shall be last (Luke 13:30). With this in mind, we should pay close attention to the last thing Jesus said to us and make that our first priority. This is exactly what my spiritual son, Evangelist Charles Blackshear, has done!

Let's take notice of the closing words of Jesus in Matthew 28:19–20:

> *"Go ye therefore, and teach all nations, baptizing them in the name of the Father, and of the Son, and of the Holy Ghost: Teaching them to observe all things whatsoever I have commanded you: and, lo, I am with you always, even unto the end of the world. Amen."*

Ever since knowing Charles Blackshear from high school, I have found him to be a bold, audacious witness for Christ. He has lived with a passion to know Christ and to make Him known. He has unashamedly shared Christ with his schoolmates, his family members, his neighbors, college schoolmates, homeless people on the streets, gang members, drug dealers, and even corporate executives.

This is a passionate book, filled with riveting testimonies and encouraging examples of boldly working to fulfill the Great Commission given by our glorious Lord. Timidity has no place among those who know Christ. We are called to reach the lost and teach the found. Now is the time!

It is sad that the world has a lie but tells it so well, while the church has the truth but tells it so poorly. If a person believes a lie, he will live a lie. But truth has the power to set every captive free. We cannot afford to be silent in the day of good news!

This book will challenge you to be more and do more for Jesus Christ, remembering that ultimately only what you do for Christ will last! This book will encourage you, equip you, and empower you to win the lost at any cost. Its brilliant content will cause you to be armed and dangerous to every demonic ploy on the earth.

It is past time for the believers in Christ to awake from their slumber and be charged to do their part in fulfilling the Great Commission. You will finally develop the courage to jettison every excuse that has held you back from making a bold impact for Jesus! **Let the journey begin...**

Acknowledgments

To my wonderful Savior Jesus, I love and worship You eternally. Thank You for Your sacrifice on the cross of Calvary on my behalf even though I didn't deserve it. Thank You for preserving me for this moment and this hour. Help me to seize this moment fully for Your glory alone!

My sincere appreciation to Betty, my beloved wife, my best friend, and most faithful supporter. You never even once gave up on believing in me, even when I doubted my own self at times. You've never spoken a negative word against me, but always spoke life into me even in the darkest situations. You've always had my back, no matter what circumstances we've gone through. My life is complete and full of joy because of you, my dear. You continued to push me to finish this book, so this one's for you, Betty. I will forever love you, sweetheart!

To my precious mother, Ruby Leola Crawford Blackshear: Mother, you sacrificed in giving everything you ever had to your three children. You prayed relentlessly for me to be the man of God that I've become. And even though you're at home in the arms of our beloved Savior Jesus, your prayers that you prayed while down here on earth are still being answered to this very day. Thank you for setting such a high example of a praying woman of God. I'll always love you, Mother.

To Bishop Bronner, my spiritual father, my pastor, my confidant and friend. You and I both know that you were totally the inspiration for this, my first book. Bishop, I so honor and appreciate both you and your wonderful, lovely wife Dr. Nina. I respect you for your guidance, love, impartation, and overall patients with me over these thirty-eight-plus years. You have poured into me and invested so much in me as a father in the Lord that mere words cannot adequately describe my adulation and sincere love for you, sir. Thank you for pushing me to go after every single thing that our precious heavenly Father has in store for me. When other books come out of my spirit then, Bishop, Jesus used you to get this whole train rolling!

Thank you, Mama Naomi Williams, for consistently having our backs in prayer. Thanks for your love, support and encouragement which means a lot to us, along with your positive attitude of a true warrior for Christ. Betty and I love and appreciate you so much for speaking life over us all of these wonderful years.

To my Uncle Clarence and Aunt LaVern, I love you both; you're the only parents Betty and I have now. Thank both of you for your love and support.

Much love, appreciation, and thanks to Deacon Edward Artis and your lovely wife Lottie for your support and prayers in helping me complete this project through a very arduous time.

I would especially like to thank Angelique McMath Jordan, for doing such an outstanding and professional editorial job. You are like family, Angelique. Thanks to the wonderful people at Editor World, especially Kristen Stieffel for your expertise in getting me out of a jam at the last minute. Thanks to all of the wonderful people at WestBow Press who put this whole entire book project together. You guys did a well-done outstanding job!

Introduction

Have you ever wondered why some churches are packed to the brim and other churches are struggling just to keep the eighteen members they already have? Does this happen by accident or is this intentional? How does one start with eighteen members and multiply to over five thousand members in a relatively short period of time? Is this sustained growth, or is it just hype that will eventually fizzle out? Is it true that a congregation can only grow to the level of the knowledge and experience of its pastor?

Do you have a desire to win the lost, but you're apprehensive because of your lack of experience in not knowing what to say or how to strike up the conversation? Do you have an overwhelming desire to become extraordinary and to do great exploits for the Lord instead of being an average, dull, mundane, boring Christian? These questions, along with many more, will be answered in the following chapters.

This book is, without a doubt, indeed a book of action. As you read these pages, you'll discover that this book is for struggling pastors who need help, pastors who want to see exponential growth in their churches, young evangelists, washed-up leaders, mundane and mediocre Christians, burned-out preachers, and desperate believers who want to be on fire with a passion in their hearts to be effective soul winners. To sum it all up, this book is for people who want to put an end to plain simple boring church as usual, and want to see **an evangelistic explosion of the power of God the old fashioned way!**

I must give you fair **WARNING:** the principles and truths discussed or revealed in this book, when applied correctly, will cause immediate, evangelistic, explosive, undeniable life-changing results in just a matter of a few months. The question is, are you prepared for such massive results? Is your church prepared and equipped for such radical changes? What will you do and how will you respond when a growth explosion takes place in your church? There is absolutely nothing worse than a golden, God-inspired opportunity that presents itself, but because of lack of preparation, we are unable to effectively handle the opportunity that awaits us and, as a result, have to let it pass us by. But with proper training, anticipation, and expectancy, you and your congregation will be on the cutting edge of what the Lord is doing in the local church today: **intentional evangelistic outbreak.** Even if you're not a pastor, but a believer who has a desire to see the world taken over by the Lord, then **get ready to be set on fire yourself!**

CHAPTER 1

No Questions Asked. Just Do It!

W ho would ever have dreamed that three young, inquisitive teenagers would finally make their way up the spiritual ladder only to be used by the Lord worldwide? Those teens included my brother, Thomas Blackshear, who is one of America's top African American artists and illustrators; one of my closest friends, Kenneth Bentley, who is one of the country's top bass players and an evangelist in his own right, and me. There we were, down on our knees on red, yellow, and brown strands of twisted shag carpet in the living room of my family's apartment at London Town Houses in Atlanta. As we knelt down and talked to Jesus in prayer, I specifically remember asking the Lord questions like, "Lord, will I be used by You to bring deliverance to individuals in an awesome way? Will You empower me with miracles, signs, and wonders in my ministry?" Additionally, my brother Thomas would ask, "Lord, would You anoint my hands to such a degree that my paintings are known worldwide to bring glory to Your name?" And Kenneth would ask, or shall I say describe, to the Lord the type of young lady that he'd like to meet and marry—

her weight, size, skin complexion, beautiful looks, and her unwavering faith.

Well, that was thirty-five years ago. All of the above has come to pass and more, beyond our expectations. Immediately after that prayer, Kenneth and I would walk up and down many streets of Atlanta preaching the gospel with power and passion like two young lads shot straight out of a cannon. We would minister to anyone who looked like, talked like, or even walked like a human. I would marvel at how God would use Kenneth to explain real-life problems and their solutions to the unsaved audience. He would quote parables from the Gospels and apply them to the world today, and not even stammer as he explained with precision and clarity the infallible word of God. We had such boldness and fire that one would have thought we were being paid a hefty fee to do what we were doing with such ease. However, that was a far cry from the truth. No one paid us, no one coerced us, no one twisted our arms. It all came from an encounter with the Master Himself, Jesus! This was the result of our spending precious time on our knees and talking to the Lord. In essence, one can only have total success after spending time on his knees before the Lord in prayer.

Today's Christians, in comparison to those of yesteryear and in comparison to those mentioned in the book of Acts, are so different one would suspect that modern-day Christians have started a whole new religion. Along with fly-by-night trends such as secular humanism and the new age movement, Christians who are complacent, apathetic, and pompous talkers who show absolutely no actions in their walk with the Lord would keep Satan content.

Unfortunately, many modern-day Christians have been lullabied asleep, like Samson on the lap of Delilah. We rest in the comfort of that favorite pious statement, **"I choose not to preach the gospel down one's throat, but I let my life be a silent witness to those around me."** Good try, but what a cop out!

Don't let me confuse you when indeed our lives are to be

silent witnesses for the most part, but there are times that the Lord will set up divine kingdom appointments that are assignments for you, and you alone, to fulfill. Many times this requires your befriending that person and disarming him to a degree that will give you a platform to minister to him about the love of Jesus. You do this in wisdom by knowing when and when not to open your mouth. *"He that winneth souls is wise"* (Prov. 11:30). In other words, there are times you must OPEN YOUR MOUTH AND VERBALLY WITNESS ON BEHALF OF THE LORD!

Jesus made it crystal clear in the Bible when he tells us in Matthew 28:19–20 to *"Go ye therefore, and teach all nations (make disciples of all the nations, ASV) baptizing them in the name of the Father, and of the Son, and of the Holy Ghost: Teaching them to observe all things whatsoever I have commanded you: and, lo, I am with you always, even unto the end of the world. Amen."*

This is what is called the Great Commission. It is further corroborated in Mark 16:15–20, where Jesus instructs us to *"preach the gospel to every creature."*

Let's go back and look at the first-century church, our foundation as Christians. After the apostles were filled with the Holy Ghost, they began to evangelize—to share their faith through witnessing to individuals about Jesus—in their communities near and farther away. No thing or person could stop them because of their zeal and earnest love for Jesus. They boldly proclaimed the gospel of Christ in a blaze of glory, not even counting the cost or the consequences of what might happen to them. In Acts 5:40–42, the disciples were beaten for Jesus Christ and came away from the presence of the council rejoicing that they were worthy to suffer shame for the sake of Jesus' name. Can you imagine that? We modern-day Christians get upset over people laughing at and mocking us because of our stand for Jesus until we almost want to quit jobs, schools, and even move out of our communities due to the pressure of ridicule. So to avoid confrontation, we just lullaby ourselves asleep with that old comforting statement, **"I'll just let my life be a silent witness to those around me."**

Jesus commands us to "Go ye into all the world and preach the gospel (or good news) to every creature." In all honesty, about 80 percent of all churches probably do not follow this command. We have become so politically correct we do not want to offend anyone.

As we read in Hebrews 11, known as the Faith Hall of Fame chapter, we see powerful, non-compromising, dedicated men and women of God who stood on God's word of promise and as a result, powerful and miraculous deliverances occurred. But we also see a remnant of people who did not love their lives so much as to allow pleasures and selfish desires to come before Almighty God. Instead, however, they shared the joy of the Lord with everyone who came before their presence and as a result were mocked, whipped, imprisoned, stoned, sawn in half, slain with swords, as well as impoverished, tormented, and afflicted. Yet Paul said the world was not even worthy of these. Why did they do it? Why were they so zealous? It was because of the "Go ye" command of the Lord Jesus that they lovingly obeyed even until death.

For the most part, our twenty-first century American church has never had the pressure of living our Christian lives in secret to the point of our dying if we share the love of Jesus. That is, not yet. But times here in America are getting more difficult than ever before. In this twenty-first century, however, third-world countries are experiencing brutal dealings of martyrdom—even in biblical proportions. Many innocent people are put to death just because of their Christian beliefs, from China, where the church must operate underground, to parts of the world like Pakistan, India, Russia, and other regions, where people are beaten or murdered just because they decided to denounce Islam, Communism, or other gods. While in these third-world countries lives are taken on a daily basis, in America, our absolute worse punishment might be the loss of a job.

Because apathy has settled into the hearts of many American churches, when it comes to reaching the lost, we have it in our minds to "just pray for them." After all, with everything going on in the church and the Christian community, "Heck, they pretty much won't even hear what I've got to say anyway." So with this in mind, **"I think I'll just let my life be a silent witness to them."** This is often the thinking of an ordinary, jelly back, mediocre, run-of-the-mill Christian. Man oh man, don't we have enough of them already? Meanwhile, Satan is steadily rocking the contemporary Christian asleep while sin is running rampant in the world.

Listen, as songwriter Keith Green put it, **"the world is sleeping in the dark / that the church just can't fight / 'cause it's asleep in the light."** A word to the wise: *"Awake, thou that sleepest, and arise from the dead, and Christ shall give thee light!"* (Ephesians 5:14).

Unfortunately, some pastors are content with just the handful of members they have and are very comfortable with their success in ministry. They hate the idea of "megachurch growth." To many pastors, church growth brings much more responsibility and multiplied problems. This takes the average pastor out of his or her comfort zone completely. The problem with a pastor who thinks so very small is that he or she is in absolute violation of the perfect will of God. The great commission is to "Go ye..." **This is a command of God, not an option.**

Keep in mind that in the Old Testament, there were two main types of sins that the Lord pointed out: **sins of commission and sins of omission.** Sins of commission were sins either committed in the mind, body, or with the heart. *"Keep thy heart with all diligence, for out of it are the issues of life"* (Proverbs 4:23). Sins of omission were those things that the children of Israel were commanded by the Lord to do, but they neglected or omitted to do them. Sin is sin in the sight of the Lord, whether commission or omission. All disobedience is sin. Therefore if we, for whatever reason, justify our excuses for not sharing Christ with the world around us, then undoubtedly we have committed the sin of omission—that is, omitting to do what the Lord himself commanded for us to do by way of the Great Commission. Therefore, pastors who have tiny congregations that have been in the same shape for many years are completely disobeying the charge of the Lord to "Go ye." Instead of this being the Great Commission, religious churchgoers have debased it to the **"Great Omission,"** resulting in the sin of omitting to do what the Lord has *commanded* us to do.

How can an individual read this Scripture and completely ignore it as if to say, "This Scripture does not at all pertain to us?" Smooth-talking preachers can even interpret this Scripture some type of way and make it seem as if it doesn't even apply to the modern-day, New Testament church at all. How can one be so easily deceived when Jesus made the command so simple and clear that even a child could understand it with full clarity? Our instructions from the Lord are very clear according to Matthew 28:19, *"make disciples of all nations."* Just the mention of the phrase "make disciples" shows us without a doubt that this is indeed a process and not just an overnight quick work. To make something or someone denotes a process of preparation and training. **Hence, our primary goal is threefold: win them, teach and train them (discipleship), and then send them.** All of this can be interpreted as "making disciples" to the fullest extent. So in essence, the Lord commands us individually to share Christ with the world, and then to teach and train each one who accepts Him. Then he or she will duplicate the process by making disciples of others. If done right, this could spread like wildfire into a massive worldwide revival. Moreover, no demon in hell could stop the multiplication process with the Lord at work through yielded and obedient vessels.

This is easier said than done!

Let's be real about this, without pretense. One of the number one fears facing most people is the fear of standing and speaking before a crowd. Even if it may not be a crowd, but just one or even two, this still takes nerves of steel to be able to share one's faith openly with a total stranger or even a friend, because now they see this other side of you that tends to make them uncomfortable. Because of these feelings that we know people are struggling with, we feel a bit apprehensive or even embarrassed. In the back of our minds, we think, *Who am I to tell anyone about Jesus, especially when I don't have my act totally together?* or *Now that I'm sharing Christ with them, I will be the butt of all jokes and called the "Holy and Perfect One."* There is even the fear of losing friends and ending up all alone, as if you're the "freak" in the office, community, class, or the "holier than thou" person. Not to mention that, now you've shared your faith, they will watch your every move under a microscope to see if you slip up in any way just to call you a hypocrite or a fake Christian, as if you were supposed to be perfect. Why would the average person want to sign up and volunteer to be the freak show of the day, the week, the month, or even the year?

Keep in mind, every Christian must face the fact that these uncomfortable feelings are indeed real. This does not mean that one is ashamed of Christ, but it does mean that this godless society in which we live today would rather embrace evil over good—as if good and Christianity spoil all of the fun of the evil and daring illicit acts of today's society. Anyone would feel a bit apprehensive about sharing a powerful truth of the good news that Jesus is a loving and forgiving Savior regardless of whatever we might be going through in this life.

The Bible tells us in 2 Timothy 1:7, *"For God hath not given us the spirit of fear; but of power, and of love, and of a sound mind.* " Along with this Scripture, the Lord reminds us in Proverbs 28:1, *"The wicked flee when no man pursueth: but the righteous are bold as a lion."* The apprehension comes from the pressure of an evil and corrupt social order that Satan, the god of this world, is behind. You are not at all politically correct if any hint of the name of Jesus is mentioned directly or even indirectly in our world today. This is why it takes a Holy Ghost boldness, which God will supply to all who are willing to sign up for such a task, and which the Lord Himself made into a commandment according to Matthew 28.

Even if we feel unworthy, without knowledge in this area, unqualified, outnumbered, or unequipped, all God wants from us is a willingness to be obedient to His voice and simply available for Him to use us. The rest is totally up to the Father to fulfill through our hearts that are open to His will. Now please understand that every person you'll ever meet in life is not at all to be ministered to or witnessed to, unless the Lord leads you by His Spirit—sort of like a personal assignment. However, the more willing and open you are as a vessel of the Lord, the more clear and concise the voice of God becomes to you on a consistent basis.

So get ready, child of God, you're about to release supernatural power you never thought you had inside you. Get ready for the Lord to tap into the power source of your life. Keep reading, because you're about to be changed in a radical way. He will lead you into proper training, such as the contents of this book, so that when all is said and done, you will be totally equipped, ready, and mobilized for His use.

CHAPTER 2

Apathy or Indifference:
The Cancer Cell of the Body of Christ

Satan has a tool in his arsenal of weapons, and he's really been making good use of it especially here in America. Even though it is said that 95 percent of the world's evangelists have come from America, now America is in need of evangelists from other nations whom we have trained to come back to revive America, because we are in a serious backslidden state and don't even know it, or we just don't care that we are. The tool the Devil uses against our nation, especially in the churches, is the spirit of apathy. People just don't care much about anything anymore, unless it directly affects their own comfort zones. I can't think of anything more insidious, deceitful, or destructive than the spirit of apathy. It causes depression, it stifles our creativity, it stunts our spiritual growth, and it drains our energy. It can take hold in every area of life where we allow it to grow, and it can completely immobilize us. Apathy can affect us all, no matter what age, regardless of our education or income level. Kids stop caring about their schoolwork, ignore their parents' rules, and show a lack of respect toward them. Apathetic teens tend not

9

to care about much at all these days; they have a "whatever" type of attitude. Employees can be indifferent about the quality of their work and the level of their service toward their jobs, the wealthy are unconcerned about the poor, and the poor are indifferent toward the wealthy.

Nowhere is apathy more evident than in the American church today. Those who call themselves Christians can often be the most difficult people in the world to motivate. The Scripture in Revelation 3:20 says, *"Behold, I stand at the door and knock. If anyone hears My voice and opens the door, I will come in to him and dine with him, and he with Me."* And verse 22 says, *"He who has an ear, let him hear what the Spirit says to the churches"* (NKJV). That's a solemn statement. As Christians, we have gotten really good at ignoring the one at the door. That's our whole problem as the body of Christ, or the church: we don't listen anymore. We're busy with our own lives and interests, and can't be bothered. But God doesn't force His way in. He doesn't break in and enter, He simply knocks. So it is up to us either to open up the door of our hearts and allow Him to bless us and others through us, or to decide otherwise, which will lead to alienation and our ultimate destruction or demise as a church. If we open up the door of our hearts and turn to Him, the Holy Spirit will break the spirit of apathy that has taken up residence in us, bring back our motivation, and get us moving again toward the things that glorify and please our Lord. But we can't expect the Holy Spirit to do this for us if our doors remain closed. Again, He doesn't force His way in; He's a gentleman, He simply knocks. Our job as the church is to open the door of our hearts widely and joyfully let Him in.

Apathy, by definition, is **absence or suppression of passion, motivation, emotion, or excitement. Lack of interest in or concern for things that others find moving or exciting.** Indifference: **little or no concern.** If apathy had a voice, it would sound something like this:

I don't want to get involved.
That is none of my business.
That doesn't concern me.
That's not my problem.
I try to stay out of that sort of thing.
Too bad for them.
I feel sorry for those people.
Better them than me.

It's a silent and slow killer, and it is literally taking over the body of Christ like cancer takes over a human body. Matthew 24:12 says, *"And because iniquity shall abound, the love of many shall wax cold."*

Growing up in the '60s and '70s was quite different in comparison to growing up today. In fact, it was so different it's almost like comparing night with day—there is almost no comparison at all. Kids would come outside like one big happy family and simply play. We played games that would involve the entire neighborhood: games like hide and go seek, red light, and tag, just to name a few. We were very creative with our hands and would make toys out of skates, such as homemade skateboards. Bicycle spokes were used to make little guns that would pop. Now we didn't shoot anyone with these to hurt anyone because they were not that type of gun. We'd take the red tip from a match along with a tooth pick and stuff its contents down the open end of the spoke broken off of a bicycle wheel, and light the end of the spoke with a match and when it got really hot, it would shoot out the toothpick with a pop sound. Wow! What fun we had! Our neighbors were a part of our lives when it came to our upbringing. Everybody knew everybody else, and we could easily borrow cups of sugar or milk from the neighbor across the street or next door without any shame or embarrassment.

However, an enemy would move in over the next few decades called "apathy," which would cause a selfish type of atmosphere to permeate the entire community and cause kids to not want to come out and play as a group. Instead, kids are content to sit in front of the television or computer all day long and are unconcerned about mingling with other kids to have fun. New neighbors would move in, not knowing anyone in the community, and not caring to know them in any way. The very thought of a neighbor coming over to borrow sugar might create a war with this unconcerned new neighbor, because of an apathetic heart of indifference that the enemy has sown. This type of attitude would spread out all across the neighborhood, community, city, state, and ultimately the entire nation. One generation would look back and say with regret, "Wow, I surely do miss those good old days," while a new generation steps up to the scene to say, "Man, I really love my PlayStation, and wouldn't trade it for the world." *"Because iniquity shall abound, the love of many shall wax cold"* (Matthew 24:12).

Illustrations of Apathy or Indifference

Kitty Genovese was the young woman who was murdered in a New York residential section while at least thirty-eight neighbors watched from their windows. During the course of the thirty-minute assault, no one even telephoned the police. Studies have uncovered some surprising facts about these people. Interviews revealed that they were not totally indifferent, as many had suspected. The main reason nobody did anything was that each person thought someone else would take the initiative to get help. **How true this illustration is when it comes to Christianity and winning the lost to Christ.**

In *Nature*, Ralph Waldo Emerson said, "If the stars should appear one night in a thousand years, how would men believe and adore, and preserve for many generations the remembrance of the city of God which had been shown!" Warren Wiersbe, in his book *God Isn't In a Hurry*, notes that this means "We have seen the stars so often that we don't bother to look at them anymore. We have grown accustomed to our blessings." Is this true with your teens? Are they getting bored with God?

A professor gave a subject for composition class. The subject given was the word "what." For an hour, the whole class expanded and defined this word and related concepts on pages of paper. A mischievous student submitted his paper in one minute and left the class. On his sheet, next to the word "what," he wrote, "so what?"

Orville and Wilbur Wright had tried repeatedly to fly a heavier-than-air craft. Finally one December day, off the sand dunes of Kitty Hawk, North Carolina, they did what man had never done before. They actually flew! Elated, they wired their sister Katherine, "We have actually flown 120 feet. Will be home for Christmas." She ran down the street and shoved the telegram—the news scoop of the century—at the city editor of the local paper. He read it carefully and smiled. "Well, well! How nice, the boys will be here for Christmas!"

Dr. Ed Louise Cole said, "Bad things happen when good people sit back and do absolutely nothing."

Dr. John A. Howard said, "Truth is outraged by silence."

Reasons people are apathetic

Sarcasm and Past Hurts. Many ridicule and taunt the Christian faith on a daily basis. People who believe in God are thought of by the world at large as being stupid, silly, and self-righteously moral. Christians are forced to deal with sarcasm, and their faith is mocked. It is no fun having people use you as the butt of jokes, and it is especially bad when they ridicule your Savior. With this in mind, why then proclaim the word of God, knowing this sort of treatment awaits you?

It took unimaginable courage for our Lord and Savior Jesus Christ to allow Himself to be crucified for us. It took profound courage for Peter, knowing he would be martyred eventually, to do his preaching work to ensure that people knew what Jesus had done for us. Paul was stoned, beaten, and eventually martyred for his preaching work, but he kept at it until the very end, even writing epistles from within the walls of prison. Jesus said in Matthew 10:32, *"Therefore whoever confesses Me before men, him I will also confess before My Father who is in heaven."* Jesus also said this in Matthew 5:10–12:

> *Blessed are those who are persecuted for righteousness' sake, For theirs is the kingdom of heaven. Blessed are you when they revile and persecute you, and say all kinds of evil against you falsely for My sake. Rejoice and be exceedingly glad, for great is your reward in heaven, for so they persecuted the prophets who were before you. (NKJV)*

People who have experienced rejections from past relationships or been through situations where they've been taken advantage of financially, mentally, physically, or even emotionally often have a tendency to shut down and not even try to put forth any effort in making something work out. They may still be trying to overcome the hurt and rejection caused by such a traumatic past. Keep in mind, however, that as believers we can't afford to allow the past to hold us back. Instead, we can learn a lesson or two from the apostle Paul, who writes, *"Forgetting those things which are behind, and reaching forth unto the things which are before, I press toward the mark of the high calling of God in Christ Jesus"* (Philippians 3:13–14).

Limited Knowledge. There is a saying that goes "What you don't know can hurt you." How true this saying is, because ignorance can hold us in bondage and captivity from being set free of the truth. If we don't know the function of a thing, we tend not to give it attention and forfeit it and shy away from it, even if it could mean life or death for us. It doesn't matter because we are lacking in knowledge concerning its value or importance. Only a person who is truly interested in something will seek out more information about it, and become less and less apathetic. Many Christians are unaware of the importance of being a soul winner for our Savior. They have no idea that if we neglect to minister to a soul by means of the "Go ye" command, that we are actually committing the sin of omission from a biblical standpoint. So without the proper knowledge, we continue in ignorance, therefore we are apathetic in some things of God without even knowing it.

Lack of the fear of God. Right now, a whole new generation exists that completely lacks fear and reverential awe for Almighty God. This is due to the lack of the torch being passed down from one generation to the next. As a result, many lack the understanding and the fear of the Lord completely. It is amazing to know that the whole world can be completely lost without the Lord if just one generation refuses to pass the torch down to the next generation. In the late '60s through the mid-'70s, the baby boomer generation began to lose respect for the Lord and as a result, a rebellious movement of individuals broke out during the time of Woodstock that completely changed the convictions of our nation. All of this was due to the removal of prayer from our school system in 1963. When fear and respect for the Lord God is lost, a domino effect takes place, and people begin to lose respect for one another. The Bible says in Matthew 24:12, *"Because iniquity shall abound, the love of many shall wax cold."*

Anger and Hatred of Christianity. Many people just hate God completely because Satan *"the god of this world has blinded the minds of them which believe not"* (2 Corinthians 4:4). However, the world is totally ignorant to that fact. As a result, any one person or thing that reminds the world of God and

Jesus in any way, shape, or form is automatically rejected and even strongly opposed. So love and concern are automatically thrown out of the window and the world has a selfish mindset of only looking after number one. With this in mind, people have apprehension, or do not trust others and become selfish by nature and very insensitive toward other people. Keep in mind that flesh and the Devil are in control of this type of situation and the love of God cannot be expressed by way of the fleshly nature. It is the Holy Spirit that *reproves the world of sin and of righteousness and of judgment,* according to John 16:8. But because the world would rather walk in darkness than in the light of Christ, men and women remain in ignorance and hatred toward each other.

Laziness. When referring to a lazy person, the book of Proverbs often uses the word *sluggard.* One way apathy often occurs is when people are just too lazy to want to get involved in helping others. Sometimes in the mind of an insensitive, lazy person, it costs too much to get involved, and is a waste of precious time to that individual. It does not matter how big or how small the scenario or inconvenience might be, there are and will always be those who will not help others no matter what. This reminds me of the parable in Luke 10:30–37 that mentions the man who fell among thieves and was robbed and left half-dead. A priest saw him there, but just passed him right on by. A Levite did the exact same thing, because of his lackadaisical attitude. These were both religious men who knew better, because this was indeed part of their job description, but they both probably thought it would take too much time to stop and help a dying man in need of medical attention. So in their minds, time was more important than stopping and saving a dying man they did not even know.

Christians today know what the Bible says when it comes to the "Go ye..." command, but would rather not get involved because of laziness and not wanting to leave their comfort zone. For most believers, going to church is good enough practice.

Why go the extra mile and rock the boat in someone else's life by preaching down their throats a message they will probably reject anyhow? This is undoubtedly the mindset of many believers, but creativity, enthusiasm, passion, zeal, excitement, joy, and rejoicing all come as a result of getting off our backsides and going out to do the command of the Lord God, "Go ye…" Notice Jesus did not choose disciples who were unemployed. All his chosen disciples were already busy doing something, not just sitting there in a lazy manner doing nothing. **Listen, this may be the Lord warning many: if you don't use it, then you'll lose it!**

God Hates Apathy or Indifference

Instead of churches across America preparing and training our youth to hold all-night prayer rallies, memorize Bible verses, fast and pray for the sick and shut in, or organize street services or soul-winning events, we have reduced youth programs to amusement-park trips, bake sales and barbecues, movie nights, dance contests, sleepovers, fashion shows, and PlayStation and Wii video games. Then we expect our youth to be effective in a hostile and godless world as Christians.

People of God, something is seriously wrong with this picture! Not that there is anything wrong with our young Christians having fun, but there must indeed be a balance to life in general, especially when it comes to us as Christians facing the Devil head-on in this godless society. We must prepare this young generation to be properly equipped to face the Devil toe-to-toe with the boldness of Jesus. We live in an **"up in your face"** generation that is not at all afraid to express to you what they believe and support, no matter how vulgar or immoral it may seem. However, the Devil may be bold, but his boldness pales in comparison to the boldness that the Lord God gives to his church or Christians who are prepared to go into warfare fully armed and dangerous! Let's see what the Lord has to say about this matter in His word in Revelation 3:14–22:

> *And unto the angel of the church of the Laodiceans write; These things saith the Amen, the faithful and true witness, the beginning of the creation of God; I know thy works, that thou art neither cold nor hot: I would thou wert cold or hot. So then because thou art lukewarm, and neither cold nor hot, I will spue thee out of my mouth. Because thou sayest, I am rich, and increased with goods, and have need of nothing; and knowest not that thou art wretched, and miserable, and poor, and blind, and naked I counsel thee to buy of me gold tried in the fire, that thou mayest be rich; and white raiment, that thou mayest be clothed, and that the shame of thy nakedness do not appear; and anoint thine eyes with eye salve, that thou mayest see. As many as I love, I rebuke and chasten: be zealous therefore, and repent. Behold, I stand at the door, and knock: if any man hear my voice, and open the door, I will come in to him, and will sup with him, and he with me. To him that overcometh will I grant to sit with me in my throne, even as I also overcame, and am set down with my Father in his throne. He that hath an ear, let him hear what the Spirit saith unto the churches.*

Clearly **God hates apathy**. To the Lord, average, mediocre, or just plain ordinary is boring. God wants us to have emotions such as motivation, excitement, zeal, fervor, passion, fire, influence, impact, enthusiasm, vitality, and exhilaration as we represent Him. After all, this is a part of the character of the Lord God himself, and if we name His name and walk in His ways with just ordinary mediocre works, it's as if we've insulted the Lord and personally slapped God in His face. God hates apathetic and dead stuff. Jesus said, *"Let the dead bury the dead"* (Matthew 8:22).

Jonah was to warn the entire city of Nineveh about imminent destruction that would come to that city's people if they did not repent. Instead of warning them, he gives in to apathy and gets on the wrong boat on purpose, and that entire city is about to be totally destroyed because he doesn't care. Question: What if you were the only person on the planet with the gospel of Jesus in your heart and the fate of the entire world depended on whether or not you decided to share the gospel? What would the outcome of the world be like if we had to depend on you? If you feel, **"I'll save the whole world by spreading the good news, of course,"** then ask yourself this question: **"Am I actually doing it right now?"** If not now, then you probably wouldn't do it if the fate of the entire world depended on you. This is why the world is in the shape we're in right now! Let's get busy and make up for lost time for the Lord!

CHAPTER 3

World Gone Wild: Where Are the Sons of God?

Y ou've probably heard the saying "bad things happen when good people sit back and do absolutely nothing." How true this is. Now let's deal with the question of what causes good people to sit back and do absolutely nothing. Well, there is apathy—just not caring—which we talked about in the previous chapter. There is fear, because one may feel like he doesn't want to be the one to "rock the boat" or get involved. Then there is acceptance, which I also call ignorance. This is when people feel that the way things are is the way things are supposed to be because, after all, God owns the planet, so if He doesn't move on the planet to fix the problems, then it must be the way He planned it to be. Sadly, most Christians I have met in my lifetime think just like that. Keep in mind, *"As he thinketh in his heart, so is he"* (Proverbs 23:7).

In Genesis 1:26–28, God gave man dominion over all of the planet. He commanded mankind to *"Be fruitful, and multiply, and replenish the earth, and subdue it: and have dominion..."* Whatever happens to our planet is not any fault of God at all, but our fault as humans because we were given dominion as caretakers over the entire planet. One could actually say it this way: "God is God in all of heaven, but he made mankind the god of the planet Earth." After all, Adam named all of the animals, and God gave him dominion over all the fish of the sea, including everything found in all bodies of water on the planet. God gave him dominion over all the fowls of the air, that is, everything that flies in the sky. God gave Adam dominion over all the cattle of the earth, even the creeping things that creep upon the earth. That's everything on the earth or ground. This covers pretty much all dimensions of our planet.

With this in mind, if any negativity comes to our planet through sin, rebellion, disobedience, demonic manipulation, or by any other means, whose fault is it, mankind or God's? You're absolutely right, it is mankind's fault. As Adam who represented mankind sinned, the earth was cursed by God due to man's sin. All earth now groans as decay and erosion sets in due to the curse. After further sin, God wiped out all creation through the flood and started all over again with Noah, who was instructed to build an Ark. Mankind went on with life, reproduced and repopulated the planet in abundance. This change caused widespread overpopulation of humanity, therefore new lands were discovered and occupied by men.

Chaos Has Taken Place on Our Planet as a Result of Growth and Pollution

In 1492, Christopher Columbus set foot on new ground as part of an expedition funded by the Spanish monarchy. Indians were the original inhabitants of this region of the world soon to be called the Americas. Recorded history in these countries began. Colonies and states were formed. Africans were taken from their homes and sold as slaves in America

21

to help build this country by force. After many years, the Industrial Revolution began. Later on, many factories were built, and cities grew larger and more modern as technology increased, causing major problems in the atmosphere by which we are protected. From the early days up until the present day, we have been pounding our earth with toxic contaminants and pollutants. The Industrial Revolution caused deforesting, killing trees that exchange carbon dioxide for oxygen. Due to hundreds of years of pollution, a hole has been eroded in the ozone layer of the atmosphere. This hole is 27 million square kilometers (10.6 million square miles), roughly centered on the South Pole. That area is the size of North America.

Unhealthy ultraviolet sun rays are entering our atmosphere due to this hole in the ozone, affecting the planet's greenhouse effect and ecosystem. Heat caused by infrared radiation is absorbed by greenhouse gases such as water vapor, carbon dioxide, and methane. These gases regulate our climate by trapping heat and holding it in a kind of warm-air blanket that surrounds the planet. This phenomenon is called the greenhouse effect. This planet is dangerously affected by global warming, which is so serious that it could mean the end of life as we know it. As a result, this is what takes place on our planet: Polar ice caps are melting, which results in the unbalance of saltwater causing the ocean animals to migrate southward, causing widespread extinction of species and the disappearance of coral reefs.

El Niño causes crazy weather patterns and wildfires because of hot, dry temperatures in California, resulting in the massive spread of diseases. And to think, many people are wondering, **"Why has the Lord allowed this, and where is he now?"** But from God's perspective, He's wondering **"Where are the sons of God now?"**

Listen, all of creation is waiting patiently for us Christians to do what we are supposed to do for such a time as this: that is, to take charge and subdue like God gave us authority to do in Genesis 1:26–28. Read the following Scripture references of

Romans 8:18–23, first from the King James Version and then from The New Living Translation:

> *For I reckon that the sufferings of this present time are not worthy to be compared with the glory which shall be revealed in us. For the earnest expectation of the creature waiteth for the manifestation of the sons of God. For the creature was made subject to vanity, not willingly, but by reason of him who hath subjected the same in hope, Because the creature itself also shall be delivered from the bondage of corruption into the glorious liberty of the children of God. For we know that the whole creation groaneth and travaileth in pain together until now. And not only they, but ourselves also, which have the first fruits of the Spirit, even we ourselves groan within ourselves, waiting for the adoption, to wit, the redemption of our body.*

> *Yet what we suffer now is nothing compared to the glory he will reveal to us later. For all creation are waiting eagerly for that future day when God will reveal who his children really are. Against its will, all creation was subjected to God's curse. But with eager hope, the creation looks forward to the day when it will join God's children in glorious freedom from death and decay. For we know that all creation has been groaning as in the pains of childbirth right up to the present time. And we believers also groan, even though we have the Holy Spirit within us as a foretaste of future glory, for we long for our bodies to be released from sin and suffering. We, too, wait with eager hope for the day when God will give us our full rights as his adopted children, including the new bodies he has promised us.*

Okay, but what does all of this have to do with "Go ye…" and explosive church growth? Hang on, we're getting there. All of creation is groaning and waiting in anticipation for the manifestation of the sons of God! Groans and birth pains of the earth can be heard throughout the planet in many ways.

There are more avalanches in mountain regions occurring more frequently, and earthquakes in regions of the world that have never been bothered by earthquakes before. There earthquakes take place almost every single day in some part of the world. It is only the ones higher on the Richter Scale that are mentioned, which has become more frequent now than ever before in recorded history. We hear about floods and tsunamis more now than in history. Widespread hurricanes occur even out of normal seasons. Mudslides and massive oil spills in the ocean are due primarily to human error. Many out-of-control wildfires are common in the western states due to uncommon weather produced by the phenomena of El Niño, such as the wildfires in Colorado Springs that broke previous records of devastation and destruction of massive acreage. There have been more dormant volcanoes becoming active within the last century than ever before in recorded history. At one time, tornadoes used to cause only minimal damage due to the fact that most would reach up to a category two or three. Now it is common for a tornado to hit at category four or five, causing more damage than ever before, and unfortunately claiming more human lives than ever before. All of these things are not just merely coincidental, but are all a part of Biblical prophesies being fulfilled in the earth. The entire world is waiting with anticipation for God's people to get on the ball and do the thing the Lord called us to do, that is to stand our post, pray and fast and declare spiritual warfare on the Devil. The big question is, **where are the sons of God?**

All these are signs of the planet groaning; the earth also groans throughout by way of lack of morality, lack of the fear of God or just plan immorality.

The world has the church on spiritual lockdown! Society at large has programed its descendants to believe in false values and false teachings over centuries, and it's been done in the name of amusement, when in fact, Satan is totally behind this lie. For instance, we've allowed our children to dress up as demons, witches, ghosts, goblins, and all types of other vulgar characters for Halloween in the name of fun, when this is one of Satan's most victorious nights of celebration in the demonic world. We teach our kids to believe in the tooth fairy when we loose a tooth, Santa Claus during Christmas time, and the Easter bunny during Resurrection season. These occasions seem innocent and cute to our little ones, but clearly, we've covered up the truth. Due to the lack of morality, people often view the nativity scene, the crucifixion of Christ, and a life emulating the very character and nature of Jesus Christ as lies and fantasies instead. Rather than raising up godly seeds by teaching them to fear and revere the Lord, society calls the truth a lie, and believes this way by choice.

Everything wicked that used to be on the down low and taboo at one time is now out in the open with welcoming arms from a misguided, blind society. Practically everything has come completely out of the closet. Gothics are out of the closet, gays and lesbians have come out of the closet, unsaved bold sinners are out the closet, the new age movement is out of the closet, every detestable and diabolical demon in hell has come out of the closet when it comes to the kingdom of darkness.

Unfortunately, Christians have run into the closet and are ducking, dodging, and hiding because the world has us on lockdown. They have put Christians on lockdown because of allegations of inappropriate activities performed by high-ranking Christian leaders. The charges also include the lack of anointing, mundane worship and praise, and being ashamed for the bad name we as Christians have received due to ministers who shamed the body of Christ because of their lifestyle of hypocrisy. Other religions and cults such as astrology, new age, Zen, Buddhism,witchcraft, satanism, Armstrongism, Yahweh ben Yahweh, Christian Science, Paganism, Scientology, palm readers, psychics, and Islam have taken over mainstream society and pushed Christians aside and arrogantly said "Enough with the hypocrisy."

I've got news for you, all the earth groans with anticipation and waits for the manifestation of the sons of God to come forth. My question is, where are the real sons of God, and where are they hiding? The world is sleeping in the dark and the church just can't fight, because it's asleep in the light! Wow, I'm talking about the mighty church of the Lord Jesus Christ! What has gone wrong? Where have we dropped the ball? Drug users, drug dealers, gang bangers, porn stars, rebellious crooks, pedophiles, and every other imaginable vulgar sinner your mind could conjure up would at one time have been locked up and put away for years for just mentioning these things. But unfortunately, society now accepts, glorifies and praises these vulgarities as normal life, thanks to Hollywood and late-night talk show hosts who only add coals to the fire that is already burning out of control.

Where We Went Wrong as Americans

There is a saying that originated with nineteenth-century experiments: If you put a frog in boiling hot water, it'll inevitably jump out very quickly. However, if you take that same frog and place it in cool water, then heat the temperature up two degrees at a time, you would literally cook the frog alive. Before it could jump out, it would collapse because it was boiled to death. Our wonderful nation has been lullabied to sleep two degrees at a time by Satan, the master deceiver. Just as Sampson was lullabied to sleep by Delilah, so has this nation been lullabied to sleep by the Devil.

It all started on June 17, 1963, when prayer and Scripture reading were abolished from our school system by the Supreme Court in a ruling of 8 to 1. Madelyn O'Hare, an anti-Christ atheist, was primarily responsible for the attention the case got. The other plaintiff was Edward L. Schempp, a Unitarian whose son was in class when the Scriptures were read, and prayer and the pledge of allegiance followed. He was offended and told his parents that he didn't think it was fair to be forced to pray to a God in whom he did not believe, and the rest is history. Try going to China (Buddhism), or India (Hinduism) or the Middle East (Islam) and let them know that you are offended because they are praying to their gods and not your God and see how far you get. I can promise you that you won't get that far at all. Unfortunately, this happens only in the West.

Immediate results of the removal of prayer from schools

- President Kennedy died that same year in November 1963
- Dr. Martin Luther King was assassinated in 1968
- America lost 53,00 soldiers to Viet Nam, and another 250,000 were wounded
- Murder rate went up 100 percent
- Suicide rate went up 130 percent
- Divorce rate went up 200 percent
- Abortion rate went up 300 percent due to Roe vs. Wade

A sexual revolution was started by baby boomers, those people born after World War II, between 1945 and 1964. The baby boomer revolution escalated during Woodstock, which was the beginning of a new culture birthing the hippie movement and the flower child movement. The Beatles, Jimmie Hendrix, the Mamas and the Papas, and Janice Joplin—just to name a few—all helped add coals to the fire.

The hippie movement started a drug craze in America. LSD, reefer, cocaine, and barbiturates were prevalent during this time in America. In the '60s and '70s, being gay or lesbian was thought to be a mental condition or a disease in the brain. In fact, one was considered to be immoral if too much flesh was showing. Cursing on network TV consisted of the "D" word only.

One was expelled from school back then if he talked back to a teacher. One was thrown out of class if his shirttail was out, or if he chewed gum in class. A female who was pregnant out of wedlock was ostracized and condemned by society. A slut was considered to be a sexually immoral woman marked by society to avoid and shun. In 1965, the mat game Twister was considered too risqué. Abortions were something that people never stood for; one was looked upon as a murderer. When Elvis Presley would dance, cameramen would take camera shots from the waist up because his moves were considered too sexual.

That Was Then, This Is Now

Today, some school systems have metal detectors that the students must pass through due to gang violence. Condom machines are installed in some restrooms of public schools. Immoral behavior is the rule rather than the exception. Seventh graders are taught how to pray to Muhammad and wage their own Jihad (holy war). Students with any type of writing on their T-shirts alluding to Christianity in any way are often sent home from school, whereas if a student has vulgar words on his shirt, he is only reprimanded. Sluts are considered cool and role models for teens, and thugs are now considered as tough, rich high-baller rappers. Both groups have a major influence on young kids and teens. Rappers continue to degrade women with the "B" word and other explicit content in their songs. Punk rockers promote Satanism and send messages of hate out to all Christian groups. A virgin woman of sexual purity is shunned and laughed at by society. Reciting the pledge of allegiance is disapproved of in some school systems. Elementary school children are forced to watch school plays that portray homosexuality as a perfectly normal and acceptable lifestyle choice. Homosexual advocacy groups are accepted readily into mainstream and respected highly.

Other religions are respected and given a loud voice. Anti-Defamation League is respected. American Muslim Alliance is respected. But many Christian organizations are banned from the mainstream. "In God We Trust" could eventually be removed from the dollar bill. Christ has already been taken out of the so-called holiday season; however, the word "holy" was still there, so now it is called "winter celebration." The Ten Commandments have been removed from all court systems. Bibles have been taken off of the shelves of most of our colleges and universities. Society and the government have Christians on lockdown.

But where are the sons of God?
Where have they been hiding?
Where have they been ducking and dodging?
All of earth and creation groans with anticipation
for the manifestation of the sons of God!

Sons of God need to stop hiding in the bushes and in caves and under rocks and in closets when everything else in the world has come out of the closets. We must stop trying to be politically correct and worrying about offending folks, and step out in our Holy Ghost boldness and tell this world who Jesus is. God has your back. **He commands us to "Go ye…" Tell this lost and dying world of the hope in our beloved Savior, Jesus! You and I are his hands and feet in the earth.**

Step out of your obscurity, your guilt, your shame. God has forgiven you if you've repented. It is not the time to have a pity party now, but it's time to roll up your sleeves, and get out there on the front lines of God's army and fight. Fight for your religious freedom, fight for your family, fight for your future, fight for your convictions in the Lord. We are the church of the Most High God. We're not going out shamefully, but rather in a blaze of glory! Listen, you ain't seen nothing yet! God is saving His absolute best for last. We're a part of the "latter rain" days where there will be a revival such as this world has never ever seen. You and I are the sons of God!

We are Sons of God, We are Sons of God!

Sons of God bring back the glory of the Lord to the earth. Sons of God bring back order to the planet. Sons of God bring back healing and miracles to the earth through prayer. Sons of God bring back the morality and holiness to the earth. Sons of God bring back conviction, the fear of the Lord, revival, and security in the earth. Child of the Most High God, it's time you square your shoulders back and hold your head up high, because all heaven is bragging on you, and all creation groans with anticipation for the manifestation of the sons of God! Josiah the king was a perfect example of this. Read about his life in the book of 2 Chronicles, chapters 34–35. He cleaned house like no other king prior to him or after him had ever done, and drove sin completely out of the land of Israel, and the glory of the Lord Most High was restored to Israel. Revival broke out all the rest of the days of the life of Josiah due to his boldness, passion, availability, and conviction in the Lord God Almighty! God is calling forth a Josiah generation in this twenty-first century. Sons of God, you are armed, dangerous, and equipped, so step up to the plate, because now is your time; the spotlight in on you!

Sons of God, come forth and "Go ye...!"

Chapter 4

Getting Our Priorities in Order

There are many benefits to being born again. There are so many Scriptures that support this fact. God wants us to prosper and be wealthy even as our souls prosper. This is a part of the whole package deal of being a Christian. Every believer going places in the Lord wants all of the benefits that are due us without any doubt, I do believe. However, some churches put so much emphasis on the prosperity message that they even go as far as to say that the more prosperous you are, the more God's glory is on you, when in fact there are some very prosperous people who have selfish mindsets. Does God want us to prosper and be blessed? Absolutely, He does. But the main reason God wants us to prosper is not to give us bragging rights, but to help finance the kingdom of God. Why? So we can reach out to a lost, dying world and bring them to a decision for Christ. The money is mainly to do whatever it takes to win souls, one of God's first and foremost priorities for the world.

Remember the rich man in Luke 12:16–20, who was considering tearing down his old barns and building newer, bigger ones? God said to him, *"Thou fool, this night thy soul shall be required of thee."* What about the man who followed God's commandments from youth up, but lacked one thing? Jesus said, *"sell all that you have and give that money to the poor, and follow after Me"* (Matthew 19:16–22). Why give it to the poor? To bless them, obviously. *"Whoever lends to the poor lends to the Lord"* (Proverbs 19:17).

Winning the lost, if done right, will in fact cost big bucks. We as a church need to invest big money into soul winning to be effective, and this means doing it in a spirit of excellence, not just throwing something together for the sake of just doing something. Let's do it in a way that will bring glory to the Lord in the end. The world goes all out in excellence when it comes to presenting something they think is of value. How much more should we as the body of Christ invest in something that will have lasting effects in the end, where its fruit will remain forever even to other generations?

The modern-day church in comparison to the early-day church in the book of Acts looks better in every regard. We are better dressed, better groomed, better educated, we live longer due to better eating habits, are better off financially no doubt, have bigger and better facilities with modern accouterments and conveniences, we drive sharp, clean, new expensive cars, live in lavish houses or mansions, and even have the state of the art in technology. Yet, when it comes to passion for souls and the power of God to cast out devils, heal the sick, raise the dead, and disciple new converts, we are extremely poor indeed. Not to mention that the disciples were willing at any time to die for the Savior Jesus if it came to that. We, on the other hand, in this modern-day church, are too busy living large until we would not dare think of dying for the gospel's sake, let alone bragging that we were even counted worthy to be beaten for the sake of the gospel. This sounds absurd to this generation in comparison to those in the early church.

"Go ye..." is a priority to God. Keep in mind that this

command is the very heartbeat and pulse of the Lord. The Bible says God *"is not willing that any should perish, but that all should come to repentance"* (2 Peter 3:9, ASV). *"For God so loved the world that he gave his only begotten Son, that whosoever believeth in him should not perish, but have everlasting life"* (John 3:16). In the parable of the lost sheep, the shepherd left ninety-nine sheep to go after the one (Luke 15:3–7). The question is, If God wants these people saved so badly, then why doesn't He go out there and get these people by the collar and drag them into a church somewhere, if He really loved them that much? **News flash!** You, sir or madam, and I are the very hands and feet of our Lord Jesus. We are even His mouthpiece. **We are the only Jesus this world will ever see.** When they look for Him, they won't find a tall, medium-complexioned man with long hair, a full beard, long, white robe with a golden belt and sandals, but instead they'll find you and me sharing His love through our obedience by reaching out to this lost world. Again, you and I are the only Jesus this modern-day world will ever see. God, in fact, is more interested in our living for Him rather than dying for Him. He wants us living for the purpose of being His hands and feet extended to a lost and dying world.

Persevere and Try Again

There are many, many churches in this world and in some cases, you'll find five or even eight churches within a few blocks of each other. Some cities have so many churches within a close proximity, one wonders why a revival hasn't broken out just yet. Everyone in that area should be a Christian without any doubt. Let that sink in for just a second; all of these churches in a relatively small area, yet in many cases, crime is usually the highest in these areas. Why is this problem like that? As you read this book, I'm sure that you can think of many instances that are just like that in a neighborhood that you may be very familiar with. For the most part, though these churches exist in the community, they really don't know how to connect with the community, environment or neighborhood.

Jesus tells a parable about a great feast or supper in Luke 14:16–24. In this parable, many people were invited to come to this great supper, but as the actual time approached for this feast, many who were invited started to make up excuses. Right here at this point, we stop our outreach program in that particular area and say, "We've passed out our flyers, invited the community to our fish fry and play, but no one bit the bait, so we'll just sit here comfortably and pray for them to join the church anyway. Meanwhile, we will still have church with or without them." This is the very position of most pastors worldwide.

If you read nothing else in this book, and if you are a pastor who can identify with this illustration, then I pray with all my heart that you understand that God requires much more from you, sir or madam. Please understand, neither you nor your church are in the will of the Lord in this position at all. Notice that the parable does not stop right there, it continues. Oh, yes, you can expect many excuses and reasons people will give you for not coming to church, but keep in mind that *"we wrestle not against flesh and blood, but against principalities, against powers, against the rulers of the darkness of this world, against spiritual wickedness in high places"* (Ephesians 6:12). There are forces in hell keeping people in sin and confusion. Satan will not just give these people over to the Lord without a strong fight. Remember, he is the archenemy of our souls; he's trying to take as many as possible with him to hell. Your church is strategically planted right there in that seemingly dead-end spot for purpose and on purpose. God did not make a mistake in your being there, even if the street and the area looks deserted.

Kill Religion, and Compel Them

I can recall many years ago when I was a member of a powerful and loving church pastored by a precious man of God by the name of Bishop Victor P. Smith, who by the way was solely responsible for my being able to go to Bible college. This wonderful man of God groomed me in my early years and prepared me for ministry in a radical way. I recall one opportunity he presented to me, which was an assignment to pray about before doing because this one would require my going out of town every single week. He wanted me to fill in temporarily as pastor in a small church located in Greenville, Alabama. The former pastor there, who was about eighty years of age, was kicked out of the church because of his promiscuous ways. I told Bishop Smith in response, "Sure, I'll pray about it," knowing in the back of my mind that this was indeed not the will of God for me, especially since I would travel over two hundred miles one way every Sunday morning. Not to mention *I'm an evangelist, not a pastor at all*, I thought in the back of my head. Well, after fasting a day and praying, I got word from the Lord to "go!" I was even shocked because that was the furthest thing on my agenda. So in obedience, I went. For the next six months of my life every Sunday morning, a three-and-a-half-hour drive one way, I went.

On my very first visit, when I got to this little matchbox church that was stripped of all the pews, sound equipment including all speakers, and any and everything we call creature comforts, I was complaining to the Lord, *There must have been some type of mistake.* The former pastor not only stripped the church completely, but also even took the furnace during the dead cold of winter. To me, it was absolutely crazy that a person could be so selfish and insensitive, especially a pastor.

I remember it was so cold in that place, one could see frost in the air when he talked. Hear this: that church was right in the middle of an extremely poor residential section known for being a crack neighborhood.

Directly across the street was a funeral home, literally a house. The church was a little larger than the average dilapidated house in that community, and prostitutes and drug dealers walked up and down that street continually doing their business. The few members who remained there had for the most part left the church when the pastor was dismissed—that is, all but one church mother and two other members. So my wife and I, along with these three members, were the only ones there in this cold, dead, forsaken church. *What am I supposed to do with this situation, Lord?* All I could hear the Holy Spirit saying to the reservoir of my inner spirit was "Go ye out and compel them to come."

"Compel them to come!" (Luke 14:23).

We must not give up on people and ignore them in the community and go on with our church programs as if we are invisible there, no! Your assignment is that particular community until the Lord says otherwise. Yes, that sin-infested, godless community is your assignment, and prayer will break the back of the demonic activity that may be going on in that location, but not prayer alone. We must "Compel them to come" along with prayer.

The word *compel* means **to force or drive, especially to a course of action: to secure or bring about by force: to subdue or overpower.** The Greek word is *anankazo*, which means **to constrain by force or persuasion.** Please understand, the word compel doesn't mean that we are to force people to come to church against their will, nor do we constrain them by beating them over the head with a baseball bat, but it does mean that we are not to sit back passively and watch men and women go to hell every single day on our watch without performing an action on our part. Compel is an action verb. We as Christians

37

must give the average Joe a push or reach out with a helping hand through strong persuasive means.

Remember, an unsaved person has no clue as to how good God is to him, nor does he understand how much the Lord loves him just as he is. He has lived all of these years of his life apart from knowing God, and must be taught just like a little baby, the ways of God. Our job is to go out into the highways and hedges and compel them.

Meanwhile, one is to be the beacon of light in that community and reach out to them more than just once and not give up. Keep reaching out until they give in. Dr. Mike Murdock says in one of his books, "If you want something that you've never had, you've got to do something that you've never done, because if you keep on doing what you've always done, then you'll keep on getting what you've always gotten." This means that if you are used to doing the same old thing you've been doing but nothing is changing for the better, then by all means change your approach and do something else that will work. We did just that.

Bishop Smith gave me money to purchase folding chairs and a sound system. One of the elder members brought in a kerosene heater, which warmed that little church. Then our strategy was put in place, **"Go ye and compel them to come."** Just five of us, my wife, and those remaining three members and I knocked on every door and let the community know that a new young pastor was in town, and that we wanted them to become part of our church. We made them feel they were important people and that together, we could make that community a better place. To my amazement, we had people coming from everywhere slowly filling the little empty church.

As I ministered one Sunday, I could recall five or six prostitutes all coming in together to sit in the back of the church right in the middle of my preaching. They were dressed just like they were on the streets, but they came in. I was so overwhelmed with emotion that I got choked up in trying to deliver the sermon. I was fighting back the tears, because these were the same prostitutes that we had been working on coming to the church for over a month now. Their excuse then was that no one in this church cared for them. I assured them that those days were over and their souls meant the world to the Lord. Just think, they were in our little church; they came just as they were. Praise God! They actually came!

Then the unthinkable happened. The elderly church mother who was there when I first started to pastor stood up in the midst of the entire congregation and said openly, "You women in the back that just came in ought to be ashamed of yourselves coming into the house of the Lord dressed like the Devil. How dare you desecrate the house of the Lord like this. God is totally displeased because of your disrespect for Him!" Then she sat down as if she had just done God a service. Those young ladies kindly got up and sadly headed out one by one, but I cried out, "Young ladies, please don't go because of what she said, the Lord Jesus loves you just the way you are, please come back inside." But unfortunately, that was the very last time I saw them.

There is an old adage that says "you must first catch the fish before you clean it," which means let people come as they are, and as they grow in the Lord, the Holy Spirit, who is our great teacher, will in fact convict them of things not pleasing to the Lord in time. If your church is too spiritual or too religious to endure until God deals with that person, then sir or madam, you are probably in the wrong profession. Remember *"old things are passed away; behold, all things are become new"* (2 Corinthians 5:17). This means it is a process by which people are delivered. Some are seemingly delivered overnight, but for others, it may take longer. In fact, it may take years for some people before they are totally delivered. Keep in mind, these young ladies did not have an opportunity to surrender their lives over to the Lordship of Jesus Christ because they left before I could even give an altar call. Though the Bible says, *"Rebuke not an elder"*(1

Timothy 5:1), I must admit, I broke that rule that Sunday, because I openly rebuked that self-righteous, legalistic-minded woman who openly judged those precious women who came in the church after not feeling welcomed in the past. After I rebuked that elder openly, she never returned to the church, which to me was something worth praising God for. Religion can kill a service and can even kill a person's spirit. Remember, Jesus did not call us to be religious, but to be spiritual. After all, it was the religious people who cried out concerning Jesus, "Crucify Him!"

My whole point in telling this story is that the Word of God works if we simply do it, that is to "Go ye…" no matter how bad an area or neighborhood. Show people you care for them and need them; they'll come. It works. Just don't give up on them or let religion run them out of the church. Even though that elder woman in the church spoiled what we had worked so hard to create, the young women still came to the service to visit; though they were run out by the church mother's comments, at least they came.

In upcoming chapters, we will discuss other guaranteed means you can use as bait in getting individuals to come to visit and even join your church no matter what, but whatever you do, make sure that you kick religion out of your church. *"The letter killeth, but the Spirit giveth life"* (2 Corinthians 3:6). Remember, it was organized religion that killed our beloved savior when they cried, "Crucify Him, crucify Him." Bottom line, *kill religion* in your life, and live a godly life pleasing to our beloved Savior through a loving relationship.

CHAPTER 5

The Wrong Pastor for the Right Job

Have you ever wondered why some preachers who are extremely powerful and articulate in their delivery have no one to join their church? People buy their CDs and DVDs and may even visit a time or two, but never want to be a part of that ministry. Some are stuck in traditions, routines, convocations, or organizations with too many strict rules. Pastors must realize that they are ambassadors of God. An ambassador represents his country. He can't speak his own mind or conviction, but only that of the nation he represents. And so it is with the Lord. We are only to speak His mind and His convictions based on His Word.

What if Jesus physically came to visit churches today and sat in the back pew to listen? In some cases, He would probably wonder where He would fit in. What if the Lord wrote a modern-day letter to each church, as He did to the seven churches in Asia written about in the book of Revelation. What would He say about your church in His letter? *I know how you have such a desire to have many souls come from the north, south, east, and west to pay you a visit, but they don't know where you are located because no one reached out to them to give directions to your church.*

God wants a pastor with a heart of a servant, one who has the heart of God to go after souls and teach them when they surrender their lives to Christ. The Lord wants to raise up a qualified pastor with relevant doctrine to help shape the life of an individual during tough times. God wants one who will pour into others and who wants them to go further than he or she has gone—someone with a cutting-edge ministry on the cusp of a cutting-edge revival. The overall solution is to get the right pastor for the right job.

This chapter is not designed to judge other pastors or to demean any pastor, but rather to open the eyes of blind pastors and to safeguard and warn individuals, especially those **inviting new converts to churches that have major issues with "unfit" pastors.** Realistically speaking, some pastors have made an indictment against heaven and have had major downfalls, shortcomings, extreme character flaws, and even made mockeries against God and still operate in pulpits all across the globe. Please understand, there is absolutely no perfect church or perfect pastor; there is no such thing. However, there are pastors who know to do better, but fall short in their approach, and won't listen to authoritative advice over them, but will rather continue in the error of their ways without assessing their current situation and making improvements. This directly affects those who are connected with them and are a part of the congregation, and will ultimately cripple and even damage any new convert who may attend their church. Eventually, cases similar to these can cause extreme **"spiritual retardation"** if not dealt with in a timely manner.

If you as a pastor fall into this category, then hopefully God can speak clearly to you as you continue in this chapter. Even if you don't quite fit into any category of this chapter, you may still receive revelation that can keep you submitted to the perfect will of God that you might be whole and complete, not wanting for anything. Please don't be moved or discouraged in a negative way just because the whole world does not come knocking on your church doors to come in and worship with you and your congregation. **Understand that God has only given you a select group that has been assigned to you for a reason, season, or in some cases a lifetime in your ministry.** No matter how you look at it, no matter how large or small your congregation may be, not everybody has been assigned to you.

Some years ago, I can remember being a member of a relatively small church that started off as a result of a massive split. The pastor and the assistant pastor were not quite of the same accord and as a result, an ugly split occurred in the church. The particular pastor I chose to continue supporting started off on a high note. By this I mean that the church was a thriving church and many members started to pack the church to its capacity. This went on for a while, even though the church did not have a working air conditioning unit. I'll tell you, it was so hot in that place that I thought I had died and gone down to hell, but that did not seem to matter, because we were growing in leaps and bounds.

However, there was one thing missing: an evangelism program. Now at this point, many would wonder, "why on earth do you need an evangelism program if the church is growing in leaps and bounds?" I'll tell you why: Because the members joining the church were already Christians from the other church due to the split, and still others were friends of individuals from other churches that were also Christians. At each altar call on every single Sunday, no one came down to get saved. Months later, one or two people did come down for salvation; that was all. This went on for months. Needless to say, that vexed my spirit quite a bit because I'm an evangelist, and I know without a doubt that God commands us to "Go ye...!"

Just because a church is growing does not mean you don't have to focus on the unsaved and the lost. To the contrary, Jesus preached to the multitudes and could have easily set up a megachurch in that day, but no, He was just getting warmed up and commanded us to *"Go ye into all the world, and preach the gospel to every creature"* (Mark 16:15). Numbers mean absolutely nothing to the Lord. He wants your church to be a whole and healthy church, not just a large church. **Just because a church is large does not mean it is healthy.** After all, the church I attended was the result of an unhealthy split.

For two years, I attended Georgia State University, a campus of about twenty-three thousand students during that time. I started a Bible study on campus. I reached out to sororities and fraternities for Christ as we met every week in the chapel. One day, the Lord put a strong desire in my heart to reach the entire campus for Christ. This was a wonderful idea, **but wonderful ideas are just ideas or thoughts until one actually puts hands and feet on them to make them become a reality.** What one needs for this is a strategy. Hope is wonderful, but hope alone is not a strategy. So I met with all of the other Bible study leaders there on campus to set up a meeting among all of us. Miraculously, this actually happened, and I met with about fifteen ministry leaders there on campus. I told them of the desire I had to reach the campus for Jesus, and for us to come together to have a meeting with the students to fill up one of the auditoriums so we could inform them about the campus ministries. With permission from the university, we were able to use one of the largest auditoriums on campus, which seated about two thousand people. We bombarded the campus with flyers and posters advertising our program, and people packed the place. I allowed each Bible study group leader to tell the students something about their study group so each student could choose who they wanted to fellowship with. Afterward, I ministered a short message and gave an altar call where hundreds of students came down to give their hearts to the Lord.

Many joined my Bible study in the chapel, and as a result, many came to visit the church I attended. Only one problem occurred: my thriving church started to dwindle down to almost no one overnight. Our pastor seemed to have lost his edge. One problem was that instead of him preaching the word of God in a powerful way like he had in the past, everything began to be about him. I don't quite know what happened or why it happened, but the pastor became a dictator, and people stopped coming. He became pretty shrewd and harsh.

I tried to start an outreach program at our church, and many came from outside to get saved, but he eventually pulled the plug on this successful evangelism program without any logical explanation. He never trained spiritual sons or poured himself into the lives of others, nor did he ever encourage anyone else. It was as if he were the only one allowed to be used by the Lord in any way. My friend, this is an insecurity problem. He was everything and needed no one else to help him. People obviously knew this and one by one started to leave. To add insult to injury, once a person left his church, the congregation was guaranteed to hear a negative message about that person from the pulpit, without mention of that person's name. Needless to say, when I would win a person to the Lord, the sad truth is that I would refer him or her to another church until God gave my wife and me a release to leave this church in an orderly way. **One can only grow to the level one's pastor is on.** With that in mind, your growth is at a cap. This is when you know it's time to graduate to a different level of growth in your life.

Nothing can squash the will of God like the **wrong pastor for the right job.** The damaging effects one can experience in going to a church with a pastor not in tune with the Lord could cripple a person's spiritual walk for the rest of his life, pretty much like the prostitutes I mentioned in the previous chapter. The following is a list of personality traits pastors can possess that can destroy one's growth level in the Lord. While Jesus commands us to "Go ye," keep in mind that, after going, we must bring them into the house of God to be fed, to grow, and to be discipled.

My prayer is that as you read this chapter, especially if you are a pastor, you would please examine your own heart to see if any of these traits exist within. If so, please allow the Lord to change your heart so that when people visit your church, they won't see a personality that gets in the way of the Holy Spirit; instead, they will see a vessel of God totally yielded to His perfect will, giving God the glory. If you are not a pastor, then please, if you know of the following types of pastors, pray that the will of God be done on this earth as it is in heaven.

Crab Dictator Pastor

The traits of this type of pastor include controlling behavior, insecurity, and a fear of training others as spiritual sons, or of passing the baton to another generation, for their successors might even out-preach them and make them feel obsolete. Whenever anyone in his presence seems to get attention or kudos, he grabs the individual back down to reality like crabs in a barrel pulling down other crabs for fear that another crab will outdo them. This type of pastor becomes threatened by another's accomplishments and success. He almost preaches like "It's my way or the highway; you choose."

Some of these types of pastors are actually working on the borderline of witchcraft, which is a form of mind control and domination. This type of pastor has so much pride in him that he often wants to challenge the authorities who work above him. The sad truth is that in this pastor's mind, he is doing the will of God. His defense becomes "if people leave, after all, some people left Jesus also." The problem with this type of pastor is that he has a serious problem in understanding who he really is in the Lord and where he actually fits in His master plan. He is extremely immature in the things of God, and with this type of mentality, he will never grow to the next level, but will only remain stuck because of his pride and immaturity.

However, mature pastors pursuing the heart of Almighty God will always have a desire to pour of themselves into other vessels. To their amazement, they will never, ever diminish or run out of the anointing of God in their lives. In fact, the anointing will only get stronger and more potent and will increase in their lives even more as they pour into others. They will also always have a desire to see their members go even further past their accomplishments in life and not at all feel threatened by the success of others; after all, they would have been the ones to empower the others to succeed. God will ultimately reward them not only in this life but also in the hereafter.

Passive Pastor

This type of pastor fits the mold of the average pastor in churches across our nation, unfortunately. They don't really have a mission, plan, agenda, vision or purpose, they are just there to feel important by having a group of people under their leadership. They just roll with the punches. Many of them, unlike the dictatorial pastor, are more than fine with others taking over in certain positions or roles in the church: let's just keep busy doing really nothing. This type of pastor has no evangelism program in the church, nor is soul winning even on the agenda. Instead, he allows the church billboard to do his witnessing for him, and if no one attends his service, "no big deal, our forty members will continue on with service just fine, after all, we have been this way for over thirty-five years now."

In 2008, I led a group of thirty-six people from our church to partner with Global Partnership Ministry founded by Scott Kirby from Anchorage, Alaska. Our assignment there was to help motivate and assist a struggling ministry in Alaska. The pastor was an older gentleman with a heart of gold, no doubt. He was extremely caring, humble, and loving, but without a vision. He hoped and wished for things to happen there to lead people in the community to his church, but to no avail. He only had approximately eighteen people in a church with enough seating for about two hundred fifty or three hundred people.

Together he and I developed a plan while our group was there visiting with his church: an open cookout inviting the entire community. This took time making up at least a thousand flyers and individually inviting the community. To the pastor's amazement, the people responded to the flyer and responded to our offer. They packed the following Sunday service. The pastor was so overwhelmed, he visibly slumped over the pulpit and began to weep. He had never in his pastoring career seen that many people come out to his church. He honestly did not know how to handle this amazing explosion of growth, nor was he or his eighteen members prepared for this in any way. The tragedy behind this story is that everything was given to him and set up right before him. However, because of his passiveness and lack of preparation, he lost almost every one of those souls as soon as our group returned to Atlanta.

Sermon Thief Pastor

Some of these types of pastors are in fact some or our best preachers in the country; the only problem is that they forgot how to hear from the Lord themselves. This is sort of comical, but a friend of mine often tells me how his brother-in-law drives all the way from Dallas to Atlanta just to attend our church services so he can take back with him between forty and eighty CDs and DVDs of my Pastor Bishop Dale C. Bronner's sermons and preach them to his congregation verbatim. Well, let's be absolutely honest. As ministers we oftentimes like to preach powerful sermons that we have heard other dynamic preachers preach over the years, and if we do this on occasion, then there is absolutely nothing wrong with it. However, the problem begins when pastors give others' sermons on a constant basis. They then grow dull of hearing God speak to them a *rhema* word (a word spoken right now). What if you had an individual who was suicidal come to your place of worship, and your place of worship was the last place he stopped by to see if God would speak to him one last time before he took his life? If your message were pre-planned or stolen from another, then God would be in a bind trying to convey truth and acceptance if you're locked in on a pre-planned, stolen message.

King Saul got to the point where he could no longer hear the Lord speak, so he disguised himself and began speaking to a medium or witch, the very type person he himself got rid of by kicking her out of the land, but was now desperate to hear a word from the Lord. Eli, the priest also got to a place in his walk with the Lord to where he couldn't even hear any more from the Lord, so the Lord started speaking to young little Samuel at that time, because his ear was attentive to the Lord. **We gain by use of the things of God, but we lose by disuse of the things of God.** God wants every pastor to have an ear to hear His voice and know His voice to receive fresh, hot-baked manna delivered straight from the throne of the Lord to feed hungry congregations across the world. Remember, the very message one may have stolen from another may not at all be the same word that the Lord might want to speak in your church, no matter how powerful the message might be. It may have worked powerfully in another congregation, but may become a total flop in your church. That is why each pastor must have fresh bread received from the Lord Himself, tailor-made and ready to meet the needs of that individual church.

Flat Boring Pastor

What happens when multiplied souls begin to pour into your local church and the pastor begins literally to put almost everyone to sleep because he's just straight boring? What an insipid shame! Think of it this way: the world does everything with excitement, enthusiasm, and fun. They even pour tons of money into a project hoping for guaranteed success and are usually not disappointed. But here we are the church of the Living God, not dead, and someone who needs to hear the gospel preached to him has the unfortunate experience of having to be lullabied asleep by Pastor Cemetery. **Solution: get out, get out, get out!** I know that inevitably someone will think in a pious way, "Well, God's Word is never boring and it never returns void." True, but the vessel carrying His word sure could use a lift and a boost at times. Remember, it is the anointing of God through the Holy Spirit that breaks the yoke. No anointing present, no yokes to be broken at all. This means that people leave the same way they came in, with the same problems.

The story was told about a lady who was too expressive with her praise in a church service. The ushers and hostesses walked her outside the church doors and told her not to return to that church again with that kind of worship and praise. So she sat on the curb and wept silently as the Holy Spirit comforted her by putting His loving arms around her and saying to her, "Daughter, don't weep, especially since they kicked you out. Why do you think I'm out here comforting you? They kicked me out too!" What a shame!

Legalistic Pastor

Legalism is the principle of adhering strictly to a law or prescription, especially to the letter of it rather than the spirit. This doctrine basically teaches that salvation is gained through good works based on outward looks, appearances, and actions. These are considered to be "holier than thou" people, judgmental and arrogant in their approach. Some might even refer to them as Pharisaical religious people. Most people would from the onset think, "well these are great religious people; maybe everyone else is off on their doctrine." The problem with this type of pastor or leader is that our Lord Jesus despises religion. Religion can be defined as "man's way to get to God." Jesus hates this because it was a religious spirit that he had to contend with most of his entire ministry, that sought after his life for the occasion of killing him. In fact it was religious people who shouted, **"Crucify Him, crucify Him!"**

Legalism teaches the dos and don'ts in the church, not merely the closeness through relationship with the Lord in knowing Him fully, but rather what to wear, how long to wear it, what to listen to, etc. It focuses on women not wearing pants, or crossing legs while seated, or not wearing lipstick, makeup, or jewelry. It's about not dancing, not listening to music other than strict religious songs, not swimming or ever hanging out at pools, not to mention hanging with someone else who might be a Christian but not associated with the same church. Our Bible teaches, *"man looks at the outward appearance, but the LORD looks at the heart"* (1 Samuel 16:7, NKJV). Some legalistic churches are so stuck in tradition, they will not even allow men to hug women in church because of problems with lust.

While some people may struggle in that particular area of their lives, not all people struggle with lust, especially just from a hug. Usually this pastor is in bondage to lust himself and exposes everyone else to his sin. How hypocritical!

Imagine that, after praying hard and diligently for the Lord to lead you to the right person to witness to and win his soul to Christ, you hear he has joined a legalistic church like this. It kills everything God has freed them of. They become discipled and then poison everyone whom they confront with this legalistic doctrine and teaching. I'm so hard on this issue because this is exactly how I was taught and indoctrinated. I approached everyone with a holier-than-thou spirit and even looked down on most people as if they were automatically hell bound. Don't get it wrong. God is indeed holy and commands us to walk in holiness, but not in legalism. There is without a doubt a difference. One is ordained by God, the other is taught by man and ordained by the Devil.

I recently returned from visiting Haiti after the horrific devastation of the massive earthquake that hit that nation. There was a team of twenty-seven who had gone to help in whatever way we could. Our mission and goal was completely clear, **"each one reach one."** Unfortunately, my plan did not go at all like I had expected. Instead, there was a need for us to preach in large tents. It was regrettable that the Christians there were legalistic in their approach, and condemned sinners. Imagine that for a moment: everything you used to own is all lost, including the lives of some loved ones, due to an earthquake. Many are living in tents without full privacy, yet the churches condemn women for wearing pants and kick demon-possessed people out when the Lord called us to cast devils out of the demon-possessed. Even these Christian believers who had hardly anything left to their names were still practicing legalism in the worse sense. So, our plan was to convince them that God was a God of love and not of condemnation. Remember, you must first catch the fish before you scale it. Please steer the new convert away from the poisonous teachings of this type of church.

Flamboyant Busy Pastor

This type of Pastor is very flashy when it comes to his or her dress style. Everything outward is always in place. He likes to parade his fancy car as if it is his new toy of the month, and always gives attention from the pulpit to the financially successful people who serve in the church and have made a name for themselves. Many times this pastor may shout, dance, jump, and praise God all day long; however, not one sermon was really preached, and the confession to the congregation was "Praise God, we surely had church today." By this I am not at all demeaning praise and worship in church, because it has its place, but with proper spiritual balance. This type of pastor has a walk as if he is Mr. Important, and everybody stands in line with hopes of being his armor bearer. Ever met a pastor like this before? However, he always has a way of operating the church exactly like a money-making business instead of the proper way that it should be operated in reverence and humility. His heart is on his personal success and well being rather than the concerns and needs of his congregation. Ministry is all about him getting recognized, famous, and successful. But he has totally forgotten that **ministry is people**. It primarily deals with servants, not lords, who go forth in the name of the Lord Jesus fulfilling his word through the Great Commission.

These types of pastors are always at every conference, but no results are noticeable at all in their church. They are forever learning, but never coming under divine revelation. Their associate ministers in some cases preach more than them because they are often out of town working on multiple streams of income. They appear extremely busy and preach on the very thing they themselves are going after full force: "more money." It becomes their passion, obsession, and unfortunately their downfall.

Please avoid at any cost getting involved in such a spiritually dead pit as this. People tend to look at the personality of this individual and fall in love with a personality rather than with the man Jesus. The Bible teaches us that one of the attributes of the Holy Spirit is that *"He testifies not of Himself, but of Christ"* (John 16:13). If you see much of flesh being praised, paraded, and glorified instead of Jesus, then you know to leave such a place because neither Jesus nor His Holy Spirit are present there. Satan would love for individuals to be tricked by the deceitfulness of riches and to divert our attention from the Lord and on ourselves rather than the lost souls that matter to Christ. If we seek the Lord first along with His kingdom, all of these other things will indeed be added unto us (Matthew 6:33) without our having to go after them wholeheartedly.

Big Fish in Small Pond Pastor

Many pastors are the big fish in a small pond. In their minds, they are indeed living large at the top. In their minds, their world is big due to delusions of grandeur, but it is in fact extremely small. One has to see the big picture and get exposed to other ministries operating in excellence on another scale totally in order to understand fully. Big fish in small pond pastors need to be stretched and come up to another level. When I first went to Bible college, I thought I was so spiritual that in my mind, I was there in school to help educate other students who may not have had my deep revelations and experiences in the Lord. Wow, what pride I had! I was the big fish but in such a small pond. Over a period of months after interacting with these other new students, to my own amazement, I discovered that I was actually a novice among such great giants in the Lord. How humiliating!

These types of pastors are the ones that peak early and have a cap they cannot go above. They preach the same old messages and quote the same old Scriptures because they are at a cap. Some steal others' sermons because they are completely out of fresh material. Why? They have left their first love, Jesus. They are out of touch with the Lord and usually are prayer-less preachers. Solution: If you as a pastor fit into this category, then simply go on a good, old-time fast to get back on track with the Lord. Because of your sincerity, He'll restore all things lost.

Salvation Rut Pastor

We know the importance of salvation in the Lord. Thus, the only way men and women on this planet could ever remotely think about getting to heaven is by way of inviting Jesus Christ into their hearts as Lord and King. But if this belief were heard and taught week after week and nothing else ever taught, then spiritual retardation and stagnation in the church would occur. A pastor with this limited knowledge would without a doubt cripple the growth of a church and stifle his or her congregation from going forward in the things of God. Keep in mind that **a church can only grow to the level that the pastor himself or herself is on and no farther.** It's as if the entire congregation is stuck in a salvation rut in kindergarten without advancing to other levels. Salvation is the foundation of our experience with the Lord, but then the word of God must be expounded upon and taught so that new levels of God's revelation for our lives are discovered and achieved.

I can recall a precious pastor friend of mine who preached on salvation every Sunday. The church began to grow very fast. However, people eventually began to leave the church as fast as they came in because that was all he ever taught. Every scriptural reference, and every topic of discussion in Bible study always came back to the topic of salvation. The question remains, after getting them saved, then what? It really won't hurt a pastor if he or she enrolls in a Bible college program to further his spiritual education and growth in the Lord. Then he might be better prepared and more equipped to minister to the saints of God who so desperately need more and more teaching of the complete package deal of God's amazing Word. Let us pray that pastors all over the world would apply themselves more and more to the word of God that they might have that much more success in their churches. This way the Devil will be defeated with only one weapon, the Sword of the Spirit!

CHAPTER 6

My Personal Testimony

Our family came to know the Lord about the same time. My sister Denise would be the first one to give her heart unto the Lord, but my mother, my brother Thomas, and I would follow my sister's decision very soon. We were heavily involved in occult practices, particularly my mother. However, like most people, we thought that there was absolutely no harm in practicing these so-called "innocent vices." My mother was involved in dream interpretation and burning charmed candles, among other things. She would visit fortunetellers on a regular basis and took me with her on many occasions. She practiced with the Ouija board for nearly eight years, and because we were her kids, we could not escape being a part of all of the madness around us, sort of like second-hand involvement. I can remember several times asking her to ask the Ouija board what I would be when I grew up, and what types of grades I would make in school that quarter. That board would tell things that actually happened almost immediately in some cases just to suck my mother into continuing to work with it. She was a pro at the Ouija board. Demonic spirits would move that little heart-shaped, cream-colored device all over the place spelling out words and numbers for hours at a time. Of course we didn't know at that time that it was Satan behind the Ouija board, just like most people who buy it don't know even now. People are naive and deceived thinking that this is just a little innocent game.

Remember the movie *The Exorcist*? That movie was based on a true story, and the beginning scenes were of the young girl playing with a Ouija board. **The only way Satan can come into your mind, soul or even body, is by a door of some sort that is opened for entrance.** Open doors include forms of sin, demonic games, lust, pornography, and the list goes on. Needless to say, between my sister Denise and my brother Thomas and I, we could tell you stories for days about wild, scary, crazy, and supernatural demonic things that took place in our apartment while we were growing up. There were manifestations of actual spirit forms appearing on the curtains of our living room, loud voices, footsteps heard on the staircase when no one else was at home, earthquake-like sensations in our apartment, demons knocking on and scratching windows in our bedroom thirty feet from the ground, and even physical manifestations on my mother's body. I also experienced choking episodes in my body from demonic spirits attacking me. These are just a few of the incidents that occurred. My point in sharing this personal story is by no means to glorify the Devil and his weak kingdom, but to let you know how one or two people can make a difference in the lives of individuals who were spiritually bound and seemingly had no way out of our situation. These two persons I'm about to mention just simply obeyed the Lord and followed his great commission of "Go ye..."

A new married couple moved into the apartment complex just two doors down from our apartment. They were both Pentecostal preachers who seemed to drive us crazy continually as they expounded on the love of Jesus every time they saw any one of us. Fred and Lucille Hill had recently given birth to their baby son, Fred Jr. Lucille was always very nice, but I honestly tried avoiding her because somehow she seemed to make every conversation about Jesus. She was especially relentless in her technique of witnessing to me. She would continually share her personal testimony with me and I felt at times I was crowded by her; she discerned that at times and would pull away from me. Little did I know at that moment that God was using Lucille to prepare me for the destiny He had in store for me.

Meanwhile at my high school, there stood an underclassman who carried himself just like a modern-day prophet. He was so different from all of the other students it looked as if he had just stepped right out of the pages of the Bible. He stood tall and astute like a statesman. He had the most humble look on his face, with a pleasant smile, but appeared very shy and even childlike. He had very few words to say, but one day when he opened his mouth, I practically jumped back; I thought, *whoa!* His words were so powerful and profound when he spoke I can remember telling my mother when I got home, "Mama, there is this guy in school that talks just like God talks." My mother asked me, "and how do you know how God sounds when he talks?" I told my mother, "Well, I don't really know how God sounds, but if he had a voice it would be this guy's voice." This guy happens to be my spiritual father, pastor, and friend, Bishop Dale C. Bronner. He actually never shared the gospel of Christ to me verbally, but he certainly shared it with me through his inward witness, his demeanor, character, and example. I desperately wanted what it was that he had. He went on to start an after-school Bible study called the PTL Club, named after the PTL (Praise The Lord) club started by Jim Baker some years prior. I would invite as many students to this Bible study as possible, because I knew if they would come to hear this man of God speak, then salvation would be inevitable.

The Process of Leading a Soul to the Lord

Now, all of those seeds that Lucille had shared with me started to take effect in my spirit. Keep in mind, when you share the gospel with the people God assigns to you, some of them may appear to look or act totally untouched, but God's word never lies, it in fact never returns void. Some may respond quicker than others, but the fact is that all will respond eventually. Some people plant the seed, others water it, but God gives the increase. Those who plant the seeds sometimes want to see the harvest appear right before their eyes through an instant conversion. If it does not take place, then they feel they have failed the Lord. As a general rule, it may take anywhere between five to seven individual people to approach before one person actually makes a decision to accept the Lord Jesus into his heart. Please understand, planting seeds first requires the death of that seed. When we spiritually plant the seed—that is to say, share the gospel of Jesus—that individual must first come to the breaking of the fallow ground of his or her heart, which could take months or even many years in some cases. This is when the Holy Spirit begins to deal personally with that person to change him slowly and break him down to the point where he sees the need for Jesus to rescue him. The time period of this stage all depends on the person's willingness or unwillingness to give in.

Others water the seed. As the Christian obeys the command of God to "Go ye into all the world to preach the gospel…" he or she does not really know if he is the first one to talk with that person about the Lord or not. We just have to obey and "Go." If we are the first to talk with that individual, then we are planters at that point. If we are not the first to talk with them, but they have in fact been witnessed to before, then we are watering the seed that someone else planted. Each time one hears the gospel, it penetrates into his spirit-man on the inside. Even though his outward body still practices sin, the spirit man is receiving deposits of the word of God which will one day take root and cause the spirit-man to burst out and subdue the flesh man or flesh nature. At this point, that person is "born again."

As a result of Lucille's consistent planting and watering of seeds, along with Bishop Bronner's early living example, I started praying the sinner's prayer with Lucille as she lead me to an everlasting relationship with the Lord that changed my life forever. Thank God for believers like Lucille who are strong and relentless in their faith. My sister was a Christian already a few months prior to our becoming born again, but at about that same time, Lucille and Fred led my brother and mother to the Lord.

Your Testimony, The Cutting Edge of a "Go Ye..." Generation

One of the most loving and practical ways of reaching this generation and sharing your faith with another individual is by way of your testimony. Your testimony is the best way to share the good news of Jesus with another person. Remember, just as I rejected Lucille at first, people even rejected Jesus himself, so don't take it personally. How much more will many reject us? However, for every rejection, there is indeed someone waiting in the balance for you to come and share Christ with him because he is ripe and needs to be harvested for the kingdom. Please understand that your testimony is personal to you. This means that you share with another what Jesus has done for you personally. For starters, you don't necessarily have to quote tons of Scriptures to the individual you are sharing with right away; that all comes later as you grow and mature in your personal experiences with the Lord. Until then, just keep it simple by letting whomever you may be talking with know what God has personally done for you. Too many Scriptures quoted to individuals can in some cases completely turn a person off, because we are speaking gibberish to a nonbeliever who knows nothing of the things of God. In essence, the more simple the message, the easier it will be to relate to the person to whom you are witnessing.

The Word of God says in Revelation 12:11, *"they overcame him by the blood of the Lamb, and by the word of their testimony."* After Jesus taught the woman at the well, she ran back to her village shouting, *"Come see a man who told me all things that I ever did"* (John 4:29). This was her way of sharing with rejuvenation, passion, and excitement the goodness of the Lord from her heart unrehearsed. This was her testimony. Notice it was not mechanical or rehearsed; neither was it something done out of obligation or duty, but she did it because He touched her in such a way inwardly, she could not help but to express herself outwardly by telling the world. That is how it should be if we have a renewed daily walk with the Lord. I'm more convinced now than ever before that this is what the body of Christ as a whole is missing; that good old fashioned joy that exists in the Lord!

When I first got saved in the Lord, I could not keep my mouth shut because of His goodness. I was so excited about the Lord, I made up in my mind to win at least five persons to the Lord every single day of my life. So this meant that I would have to at least witness to sometimes fourteen or more people per day to meet my quota. In all honesty, this went on for at least the first year and a half of my Christian life.

Every believer has a different story to tell of the Lord and what He has done for each one personally. If you were lonely, then you'd testify how He fulfilled your loneliness by giving you a mate, if that were the case. If you were jobless, then you express how He provided for you daily without your missing a meal. If you were suicidal, then your testimony would be how

Jesus changed your mental state from wanting to take your life to wanting to live for Him. If you are rich, you may look at the Lord for stability, and that becomes your testimony. If you're sick in your body, your testimony may be that the Lord healed you completely, and if you are not yet completely healed, then you have hope that one day soon He will heal you; this becomes your testimony. You would be surprised to know how much a word of encouragement in the form of a simple testimony to an unsaved individual could affect, impact, or even change one's life forever.

The world wants to hear good news that is real, not phony. The miracles, signs, and the wonders are what attracted many souls to Jesus—in other words, testimonies of individuals who were healed, delivered, and set free by the power of God. One young lady in my high school saw the raw fire of God working in my life to the degree that she asked me out of curiosity, "How did you become so convinced that the Lord is even real at all?" She asked a simple question, so I gave her a simple answer: "My whole family was unsaved and involved in occult practices and Jesus caused the power of Satan to be broken in our lives so that our spiritual eyes became open to see Him as the one and only true and living God." "Wow, that's great," she responded. I led her to Jesus and had her praying the prayer of salvation in less than five minutes. When the harvest is ripe, it is that simple.

Your testimony is from your personal experiences in Christ and from your complete perspective. Jesus may deal with you one way, but another person will be dealt with by the Lord a completely different way. For example, let's say you're a young kid and your father is a very successful businessman. His peers and colleagues might look at him as a hard, stern, and even shrewd competitor, and all of this might actually be true looking at it from their perspective. On the other hand, that same man looked at through the eyes of his little child might be a very funny, goofy, and playful father who loves deeply and shows it. Through the eyes of the people of the world, God may look like the businessman to his peers. But to you as a Christian, you show the people of the world another side of your Father that they don't know about by sharing your testimony of Him; a loving, compassionate, long-suffering, forgiving, and understanding Father. The children of Israel in the Old Testament knew God's acts like the people of the world, but Moses knew the Lord's ways like the body of Christ or the church.

My Calling made Clear

The order of God is very clear. As soon as the Lord saves us through acceptance of His dear Son Jesus, God gives us our marching orders in life. Some receive them sooner than others, but we all receive our orders from the Lord in due season. I received the call of God to operate in the ministry of an evangelist as soon as a *rhema* (spoken) word came to me through a prophet of God. My mother and I attended a Pentecostal church in Decatur, Georgia, on the corner of Second Avenue and Tilson Street, pastored by Apostle Milton Perry. Apostle Perry was a short man with a big voice full of power and anointing when he spoke. That particular week, he had invited a fireball of a prophet of God by the name of Prophet Brian J. Mosley to run revival there. This man of God was dressed in all white from head to toe each night, and even wore a purple cape (one of many other colors he had) when he would move in the prophetic anointing. He was an anointed prophet on the cutting edge with a word from the Lord and a keen gift of word of knowledge (the ability to call out individuals and tell them things concerning their present situation revealed by the Holy Spirit) working in him along with the gifts of healing and miracles. At that time he was twenty-one years old and I was only seventeen. After he had preached the word of God and given an altar call, many souls came down to accept the Lord for the first time.

As the congregation praised the Lord with great anticipation and expectancy, the man of God started to operate in that gift of word of knowledge. He walked down the aisle and called a particular young man out and had him to stand up. He asked him if he had ever played the organ or piano before. The young man replied, "No sir, I have not."

Prophet Mosley then said to him, "Well young man, that is about to change after tonight. In fact, you're going to play that organ and piano like Ray Charles." After that word, the young man took off running around the church and everybody began to praise the Lord with excitement.

Then the man of God made his way down the aisle where my mother and I were sitting. As he came closer to where I was sitting, my heart began to beat so hard and loud, I thought everyone in the church could hear it beat. As my mother began to weep with excitement, Prophet Mosley called me to stand up in front of over eight hundred people. As he approached me and was about to lay his hands on me to pray, a divine interruption took place.

Everyone jumped up on one accord as the most powerful melodious sound of a Hammond B3 organ poured out from the young man as he sat before the organ. This was the young man he had just prayed for and given a word of knowledge. He played that organ like a professional and to be honest, it was difficult to believe that he had never played the organ before. This indeed was a miracle to behold. Needless to say, the church danced and shouted for another fifteen minutes or so, and my mother and I were so happy just praising the Lord.

But on the inside, I was wondering, "Lord, I hope you didn't forget about me, after all the prophet was about to pray for me."

No sooner than I thought of that, Prophet Mosley was running down the aisle this time heading straight in my direction. He stopped and said over the microphone, "Didn't I tell you all that he would play that organ like Ray Charles, Ray Charles, Ray Charles, Charles, Charles, Charles."

As he approached me, he asked me again to stand up in front of everyone. He then came up to me and asked me my name. Of course, I said in amazement, "Charles." Every one was shouting and began to praise the Lord even more.

Let me mention something to you of importance at this point. Remember, I was in high school in the eleventh grade at this time. I attended the PTL Bible study that Bishop Bronner had started in high school, and I was inviting people on a regular basis to participate in this after-school program. So when the prophet laid hands on me to pray for me, he began to prophesy over me for about five minutes or more nonstop. Among the things that he mentioned was that the Lord had anointed me in the office of an evangelist to do his work worldwide with miracles, signs, and wonders following me everywhere I would preach. He even said that the Lord was using me presently in my high school to bring souls into the kingdom by way of a Bible study at the school. Wow, talking about a prophet of God on the cutting edge. *Wow!* How timely that word from the Lord was to me. Until this present day, I have seen God at work in my life fulfilling that prophesy over and over again.

I mentioned all of that simply to say, what if Lucille had given up on me the first time I blew her off? I probably would have gotten involved with something or someone that might have caused me to lose out on hearing God's word and receiving Him into my life. My life, ministry, and even this book are all a result of someone who did not mind going out of her comfort zone with persistence to share Christ with me. What if the next person you talk with may be the Billy Graham of his or her generation? Even if he is not a Billy Graham, in the sight of the Lord his soul is worth the world.

Sir or madam reading this book, what if I had run into you with the problems my family had? Would I have been a Christian as a result of running into you? Would you have discerned my condition and known that there is absolutely no problem too big for our God to handle? Are you on your way with the Lord or are you in the way of God, not doing your job as a Christian by not obeying the "Go ye..." principle? Are you one of those who believes this command does not apply to you at all because you are not an evangelist? **Please keep reading so you may be enlightened, equipped, and even motivated to do what the Lord has commanded all of us to do, that is to "Go ye...!"**

CHAPTER 7

The Spark Is Motivation

In this chapter, I would like to introduce to you a life changing word that you may or may not have heard before. There is also another word that is the exact opposite of this word that I will talk with you about as well. You can say that one word is inspired by the Lord, and without a doubt, the other word is inspired by the wicked one, Satan. The great thing about our God is that He has given mankind free will to choose anything we want in life. **You and I are the sum total of all of the decisions we have made in our lives up to this present point.** With that in mind, if you don't like the direction your life has taken thus far, then from here on, make better and right decisions for your life. Yes, no matter how young or old you may be or how majorly screwed up your life might be currently, there is still time left to change your present and secure your future just by making right choices from here on out.

The disciples made a choice to follow the Lord Jesus no matter how difficult their pending fate may have been. The Bible says, *"they loved not their lives unto the death"* Revelation 12:11. This means they were literally willing to lay down their lives for the cause of Christ, the one they believed was the Son of the living God. This attitude infused the disciples to go on with their witness for Jesus even farther than ever before.

I first heard of this word that I'm about to introduce to many of you from a friend and a mentor of mine and one of this country's most outstanding **evangelists, Mario Murillo.** My wife, Betty, and I had the privilege of being a part of Mario's soul-winning conference in San Francisco. We participated for two consecutive years and became close friends with him up to this present day. God had given Mario a breakdown and revelation of this word that I have never heard of before or since. I'd like to share this revelation with you.

This life-changing word is **"conation."** Now, if you try looking this word up in a pocket dictionary, well, good luck. You won't find it except in collegiate and unabridged dictionaries. *Conation* **is the area of one's active mentality that has to do with desire, volition, and striving. It is the energy of the mind which produces an effort. It is also the process by which thought is turned into action.** If we expound on this word from the aspect of the Holy Ghost, then it is a violent, God-given drive to succeed in pursuit of a divine goal. It doesn't back down, back up, back off, or back away! It says, in essence, my mind is made up; you will have to kill me to stop me. It is raw, holy enthusiasm, excitement, dynamic drive, and fire in the bones. It is pure initiative that propels someone into a single-minded pursuit of a vision. Conation is indeed the spark in motivation that every living Christian must have in order to be successful in soul winning and in fulfilling the Great Commission of the Lord.

Examples of Conation

The Disciples. Conation made the disciples say, *"We would rather obey God than men,"* (Acts 5:29, 40–42) after being savagely beaten simply for preaching the gospel of Jesus Christ. They were forbidden and even told not to continue in this manner of teaching or else it could mean death for them the next time. Do you think that stopped them? They were even more radical and unstoppable because of the threat.

Esther. Conation caused Esther to go before King Ahasuerus uninvited, knowing that death awaited her if the Lord would not intervene. Along with all of Israel, she fasted and had Mordecai, her uncle, fast and pray for her. She said to Mordecai in words of bravery because of the conation that had set in, *"If I perish, I perish"* (Esther 4:16). Wow, what a champion for the Lord. As a result, the king extended the golden scepter unto her, something that was totally against all protocol back in that day, and needless to say Esther's request of the king was granted unto her.

David. Conation caused a little shepherd by the name of David to go up against a giant by the name of Goliath who had taunted the entire army of Israel for weeks. All of Israel was at their wit's end because this larger-than-life giant couldn't be defeated by anyone; that is, except for a God-fearing David, in whom conation had set in full force. His mind was made up to where it couldn't be changed, because he remembered what God had done in the past when a bear and a lion came to attack the sheep for which he was responsible. David broke the jaws of lions and bears with his bare hands because of the anointing of the Lord upon him. David told that giant, as he faced him without armor and with only a slingshot and five smooth stones in his hands, *"Thou comest to me with a sword, and with a spear, and with a shield: but I come to thee in the name of the LORD of hosts, the God of the armies of Israel, whom thou hast defiled. This day will the LORD deliver thee into mine hand, and I will smite thee, and take thine head from thee; and I will give the carcasses of the host of the Philistines this day unto the fowls of the air, and to the wild beasts of the earth; that all the earth may know that there is a God in Israel"* (1 Samuel 17:45–46). To stop David at this point, one would have had to kill him. However, he did just what he told Goliath he would do to him. David knew how to get a "head" in life—pun intended.

Stephen. Stephen was a mighty man of God whom the apostles had chosen to do the work of a deacon. His story is found in the book of Acts, chapter 7. His life is an example of conation kicking in because he had faced the entire Jewish council, which would be like facing the Supreme Court in our modern day. They had lying witnesses to testify against Stephen, saying that he had spoken against the temple and against the laws of Moses. Now Stephen could have easily talked his way out of the charge against him, but because of conation, he stood strong and bold on behalf of the Lord Jesus, knowing that death was imminent. He died as a martyr for the Lord, stoned to death for his undying, bold, committed faith in the Lord.

Rosa Parks. This is the African American woman who sparked the civil rights movement in the early '60s. She refused to give up her seat on a bus to a white person when she had worked hard all day and was extremely tired. She knew that the consequence for her refusal back then during segregation was to serve jail time, but because conation set in, she was determined to remain seated until policemen removed her from the bus and escorted her to jail. Her mind was made up without a doubt regardless of the consequence. Conation doesn't care about consequences. It is raw, holy enthusiasm, dynamic drive, and fire in the bones. "To stop me, you have to kill me."

Pastors Please Take Note: Your Church Is Only as Motivated as You Are, No More.

My pastor, Bishop Bronner, always quotes "motivation is what gets you going, but habit is what keeps you going."

Unfortunately, many pastors think like this when it comes to winning souls for the Lord: "My people are not used to going out there doing this sort of thing," or "It's pretty hard to get my people interested in something they are not used to doing." Well, the question is, whose fault is that? Your congregation will only grow to the size of its leader, the pastor, without a doubt. If your knowledge in the Lord, your experiences, and your teachings are at a cap or you're in a rut, then your church will only grow to the level of your teachings or experiences in the Lord.

Who is motivating your congregation? Many members will inevitably visit other churches on occasions and discover that there is a plethora of ministries on fire for the Lord doing what God intended for them to do, that is to "Go ye…" However, when they return to their church, which at one time they thought was thriving in the Lord, they discover how dead and dry the church really is. It is as if like Adam and Eve "their eyes have become open." How do you get your otherwise dry church to change and become motivated?

Remember, pastors, they will only grow to the level of your knowledge, experiences, and understanding. In other words, **you are the hindrance in most cases.** Rather than you removing yourself or throwing your hands up as if to say, "let them go somewhere else then," God is simply waiting patiently for you to kindly step to the side, that is to yield to Him, so He can come in to take His church to another level. But he desperately needs your help, pastor. In fact, He can't do it without your help. You are the angel He has sent to oversee the work of the ministry at your location; you just need to position yourself in the proper alignment for His creativity and anointing to flow. It is your responsibility to equip yourself and to prepare yourself to be used as a vessel of honor before the Lord. This means that it is time for you to take your walk in the Lord to a completely higher level. **No more mundane, mediocre, business-as-usual practices. It is time to upset the** kingdom of Satan and forge an all-out war on the darkness of this world by waking up and positioning your members as a mighty army before His Majesty. This will require that you spend much more time before the presence of God in fasting, prayer, continued Bible study, and maybe even going to Bible college or continuing Christian education courses to prepare yourself for the next level. This advice should not be taken as an insult, for we have entirely too many prayer-less spiritually immature preachers full of spiritual malnutrition. No wonder Satan is not threatened by the church like he used to be. Apathy has begun to set in. If the church in the book of Acts could see us today, many of the saints of old would indeed roll over in their graves in sheer disgust.

Spiritual Stagnation

In all fairness, ask yourself the question, "Why did God Almighty call me to pastor a church?" Or, "Why did He call me to preach the gospel in the first place?" Was it something to do to pass the time? Was it because God wanted me to be respected by many as being a part of the clergy? Was it so I could rule over others and feel important as one who is revered as a spiritual father? Could it be because since I'm a Christian, God wanted me to train or to disciple other Christians?" Whatever reason you might feel is the proper answer, we must ultimately consider God's answer from a biblical perspective.

Many churches, though members are represented, only fill in space and occupy precious time doing nothing but having a good time among themselves. I was a member of a church that fit in this category. In fact, this was really the very first church that I was committed to attending in my teenage years. This church was a fun type of church. This pastor was the type of minister who would often mention the names of members of the church in her sermons when she would try to make a point. She was able to do this because her church was so small in number and everybody there was like one big happy family. We had some of the best times during church functions and picnics. We would play softball, have potato-sack races, water-balloon fights, watermelon-eating contests, you name it, we did it and had so much fun doing it. We were all so close and had the time of our lives. We laughed together, cried together, shared personal information with one another, and even continued our friendships outside the church walls. Everybody knew everybody else's names and we all got along so well. When someone new would come by occasionally to visit, this was the gossip of the church. The pastor of this church was extremely charismatic in her approach when it came time for the preaching of the word of the Lord. She was also a very inspiring and challenging minister when it came to preaching the gospel. The she I'm referring to is not the same woman of God who led me to the Lord. Just thought that I'd mention that here.

Oftentimes newcomers would only stay for a while, maybe six months tops, and then leave. Nevertheless, the faithful few would always remain committed and continue business as usual. It didn't hit me until years later that God wasn't really pleased with that church at all. Why, you might ask? Because though we had the best of times among ourselves, this church was totally unproductive when it came to the affairs of the kingdom of heaven. There was absolutely no outreach program set up to win the lost, no evangelistic efforts supported, and no vision from the leadership to involve the congregation at all. I can't even remember clearly any time that she gave an altar call, because it was the same old group and everyone of us were already Christians.

Countless churches exist in the world today just like this church and have no conviction at all in what they are doing because in all honesty, in their eyes, they are doing absolutely nothing wrong. What rules have they broken, what sins have they committed, what evil have they done in God's eyes for me to make a statement such as this? The answer is very simple. It is not what they have done that makes them guilty, but rather what they haven't done that makes them guilty before God's eyes. Keep in mind that in the Old Testament, there were only two major types of sins mentioned; sins of commission, and sins of omission. Sins of commission are obviously acts of sins that are committed by an individual or a nation of people at large such as the nation or children of Israel. These sins could range from something as simple as assault to carrying out or committing the very act of murder or adultery.

Sins of omission, however, were things that were ordained by the Lord for His people Israel to do, such as participation in required feasts, or instructions concerning how to honor the Sabbath day and so on. However, if any of these things were omitted or broken, it would be as equal in the eyes of the Lord as the sins of commission because in the eyes of the Lord, all disobedience is "sin."

The other word that I'd like to talk a little about is the word *stagnation*. Totally opposite of conation, this word is one no doubt inspired by Satan to keep the body of Christ held back so we won't fulfill God's Great Commission of "Go ye…" This word means **to cease to run or flow as water, air, etc.; to be or become stale or foul from standing, as a pool of water; the state of becoming sluggish and dull; to stop developing, growing, progressing, or advancing.**

Stagnant churches are those that from the outside looking in seem to have things in place and in proper order, but are far from that when examined closely. Stagnant churches are like looking at a house that's beautiful on the outside, and when you get inside, it's even more beautiful. However, there exists heavily those little unseen insects called *termites*. Even though this house is gorgeous both inwardly and outwardly, these hidden termites in a relatively short time will consume this house from the inside out. They are hidden in the foundation of the house, working their way up to the woodwork, hidden between the walls, sowing their seeds of destruction silently. Many times, no one really knows until it is too late. So it is with churches that are unhealthy because they are stagnant.

God is about reconciling the world to himself through the ministry of reconciliation. He will indeed hold every single pastor in contempt if he is not allowing His perfect will to be carried out. If a pastor has his or her own agenda, instead of the Lord's agenda, or has a special interest at heart, then that ministry is cursed from the very roots at best.

According to Philippians 2:13, the main purpose of the church is to move with the pleasure of God. Life's greatest lessons are not learned in a course, but rather on a course. When the Lord works His pleasure in you, your attitude changes, your outlook improves, your faith is strengthened, and love and forgiveness abound. A healthy church is a growing church that is taught properly the right spiritual diet that will allow each individual to grow and mature properly in the things of God. While that growth process occurs, that individual will inevitably want to reach out to the lost simply because he has grown fond toward the heart of the Lord. He will love the things the Lord loves, and hate the very things the Lord hates and become His hands, feet, and even his mouthpiece. This is a part of the ultimate plan of God for his church at large.

Spiritual stagnation, on the other hand, denotes an unhealthy church. Even a tree branch when it is disconnected from the tree still seems to produce leaves for a while, but though it appears to be healthy, time will soon reveal that the branch is really dead because it is no longer connected to the tree. The same principle applies to stagnant churches. They appear to have things in order. People even feel that the Lord's blessings are being felt and experienced. However, if the church is unhealthy because of spiritual stagnation, then in just a matter of time, things will surface to let you know that this church is in fact dead in every way. Dead churches cannot produce life, but only death. I compare a dead church to waxed fruit in a bowl on a beautiful dining room table. It looks real and healthy, when it is only dead and fake.

Stagnation of water in a pond or a large hole in the ground filled with water breeds all types of diseases and bacteria. Even mosquitos are bred in environments where there is stagnation of some sort. The same applies in a spiritual sense as well. Spiritual stagnation occurs when there is no productivity in the same manner as natural stagnation. It breeds spiritual bacteria that cause spiritual diseases to form and grow and eventually kill off the entire flock.

This little church unfortunately had a tragic end. I don't mean to gloat or sound selfish in any way, but I thank God that He called our family away from that fun-filled church before His judgment fell on it. To sum it all up, quite a few members there died months apart from each other due to sudden sicknesses, tragic accidents, and even a suicide. Others in head leadership positions were exposed for adulterous relationships and embezzling church funds. This caused the few remaining members of that fun little church to split up and the building to be padlocked. Eventually, the church was torn down and made into a parking lot.

Two Motivations: Money vs. Favor of God

What are some things that motivate people? Well, there are always promotions, or rewards, not to mention money. Now just think for one minute. I'm sure you've experienced people who were introverted at some point in life, but they got a hold of one of these multilevel marketing companies which required them to open their mouths and try to motivate others to become a part of this lucrative opportunity that could make them wealthy. Not only did they break out of their somewhat shy demeanor, but they in fact became so motivated that one may have scratched his head wondering, "Is this the same person? I did not know he could even talk." But they did. Why? Because the idea of possibly becoming an overnight millionaire was the motivation that caused them to break out of their comfort zone and do what may have at one time been uncomfortable, but looking ahead at the reward of wealth motivated them to go there. Now what is my point? My point is that the right motivation can move any person.

What if for every soul that a Christian shared his faith with about the Lord, and in fact won to the Lord, his reward was a check for $2,000 per soul? Now let that sink in for one minute; $2,000 per soul that was led to the Lord. Listen, there would be no sinners walking the streets ever again, because Christians would come up with all kinds of creative ideas for getting people saved so they could cash in for profit. If five souls were won to the Lord in one day, that Christian would receive $10,000 in one day. Do you think that this would motivate people to go out and win souls on a daily basis? You better believe that it would!

One soul to the Lord is worth more than all the money in the world put together, but many of you are saying right now quite frankly, "Yeah, but that money would surely motivate me to do more for the kingdom." Where we miss it is in the fine details. **Favor with God** will take you places in life where money can't even go. And if we are motivated to be soul winners for the Lord, then favor is only a small byproduct of many overwhelming blessings that will follow us in life everywhere we go. The Bible says it this way: *"But seek ye first the kingdom of God, and His righteousness; and all these things shall be added unto you"* Matthew 6:33. "All these things" could mean wealth, health, good relationships, open doors that would not have been open any other way, long life, wisdom from the Lord, a sound alert mind—the list could go on and on.

Money can't compare to the Lord's blessings and favor

in our lives. It would be like comparing a beach ball to the entire planet Earth. Now if that doesn't motivate you, then your wood is indeed wet. At this point, buckle up your seat belts, because from now on, it will be a bumpy ride. Expect an individual breakthrough from taking up space, to taking off into hyperspace for the kingdom of God. **Get ready for massive soul-winning breakthroughs that will make Satan shake in his boots!**

Chapter 8

The Power Factor:
Your Undeniable Proof!

In this chapter, several questions will be answered in regards to receiving the power of God in your life without measure, walking in the prophetic call and purpose for your life specifically, dealing with rejection from the world, and even the benefits that your Father will bestow upon you as a result of your obedience.

In James 1:22–23 the Bible says *"Be ye doers of the word and not hearers only, deceiving yourselves." Doers* denotes action, going, movement, response, and liveliness. "Go ye…!" God commands us to move, get going, and do. Remember, this is not an option but a direct command from Jesus Himself.

People who read this may be even thinking, "Yeah, that really is what I need to be doing as a Christian." But then, that is the extent of their conviction. Keep in mind, *"To him that knoweth to do good, and doeth it not, to him it is sin"* (James 4:17). Sir, ma'am, if after receiving the knowledge of the truth concerning the Great Commission to "Go ye…" we still live our Christian lives without sharing our faith and witnessing to others about the goodness of our beloved Lord Jesus, and if we are not making disciples on a regular basis, then we have sinned before Almighty God. We continually sin as long as we are not obedient to His word. It matters not who you are, how long you've been a Christian, or in what state or condition your walk with the Lord is at this point in your life, but "Go ye..." is a command, not an option. No wonder so many Christians' lives are messed up and out of order. We are sometimes so concerned about the Lord blessing us and keeping us that we have become totally oblivious to the needs of others.

We've already talked about the distinctions the Bible makes about two main types of sins: the sins of commission and sins of omission. Sins of omission are sins that we were told by the Lord to do, but neglected to do them. Well, now we are totally without excuse because the Lord has empowered all believers to get the job done that awaits us every day. So now what's your excuse?

Staff Your Weaknesses

If you're a pastor and you say, "I don't have a musician in my church, or I don't have a choir, good singers, or even praise dancers in my church. I myself am not an evangelist and I don't have the ability to go out and win people to the Lord. I don't feel that I have an evangelistic bone in my body. I'm not wired like that, I'm a pastor and I feel the need to feed the flock after they show up for church, but to go out to get them is another story. What do I do in a case like this?" The answer to that question would be, **you must staff your weaknesses**.

What do I mean by staff your weaknesses? Pray that the Lord would send someone else with the skill to get the job done. As the shepherd of the flock, you bear this responsibility unto the Lord. If you are not in a position financially to pay them, then pray the Lord will send someone to you who is willing to work unto the Lord because of a passion and not because of money. As a pastor, you must give an account of your congregation's progress and of the assignment given to you by the Lord, presenting your congregation as an obedient church concerning the Lord's command to "Go ye…!" You must staff your weaknesses and shortcomings so you are always without excuse unto the Lord.

If you're not an evangelist, have your church pray and fast for the Lord to send you one, because His will must be done on Earth as it is in heaven. The Lord may even raise up an evangelist from within your small congregation as an answer to prayer. He may empower one from within the walls of your church with a radical zeal and a fiery heart of compassion to win souls. God still holds the pastor in contempt if he or she does not present unto the Lord a kingdom-minded church. Remember, if your call is indeed of the Lord, God will see to it that his perfect will is done in your local church. Your responsibility is to pray the will of God back to our heavenly Father so he will move on your behalf.

Dynamis Power

The Word of the Lord tells us in Acts 1:8 *that we shall receive power after the Holy Ghost has come upon us, and we shall be witnesses.* This word *power* derives from the Greek word **dynamis** (doo-na-mis), **which means ability, might, miracle, strength.** This is the word from which we get *dynamite*, which is **explosive power.** God gave and equipped us with this type of power to be witnesses.

We do desperately need this type of power to witness in this godless age in which we live. With the recent endorsement of same-sex marriage by our current president—and many churches that support his stance on the topic—along with this ungodly world trying to redefine marriage as we know it from a biblical perspective, it takes this kind of *dynamis* power to withstand in this evil day, especially when the world will reject and even try to reprimand anyone who opposes this opinion.

Think, *"the god of this world, Satan, has blinded the minds of them that believe not, lest the glorious gospel of Christ who is the image of God, should shine upon them"* (2 Corinthians 4:4). I used to think that God gave us this kind of power, *dynamis*, to cast out devils, heal the sick, raise the dead, and cleanse the lepers; but to be a witness, how exactly does that fit? All this power just to be a witness?

Our world is inundated with moral profligacy, unrighteousness, and hatred of even the mention of the name of Jesus in any way, shape, or form. Jesus knew eons earlier that this would happen to his body of believers and even warned us repeatedly throughout his famous Sermon on the Mount (Matthew 5–7). So in spite of the opposition from the Devil that we consistently face, Christ has already equipped us for such a rough task to follow. **This is exactly how it works.** Let's look at Mark 16:17–18: *And these signs shall follow them that believe; In my name shall they cast out devils; they shall speak with new tongues; They shall take up serpents; and if they drink any deadly thing, it shall not hurt them; they shall lay hands on the sick, and they shall recover.*

All of these signs are promised from the Lord to follow us. This is the key! Only if we obey the command to "Go ye!" Notice, they went. Let's look at Mark 16:20:

> *And they went forth, and preached every where, the Lord working with them, and confirming the word with signs following. Amen.*

Ooohhh! So God does give us miracle *dynamis* power to heal the sick, cast out devils, raise the dead, and cleanse lepers, but only if we do what he commanded for us to do first. Notice they went forth preaching—proclaiming, witnessing, sharing their faith, making disciples—everywhere. They completely obeyed the commandment of the Lord or the Great Commission.

As we go and obey, the Lord will indeed work with us and confirm everything that we say, share, and do as long as it is backed up in His Word, with signs following us. A "Go ye" Christian is a Christian who will see these signs and wonders working with him. Let's look at verse 20 again: As they went forth preaching everywhere ("Go ye," the Great Commission), the Lord was working with them confirming (to make valid or to establish the truth or authenticity of) the word of God that they shared to others with signs (miracles, wonders, etc.) following them as an open witness among all of those present. We honestly do not need to follow after signs and wonders. Literally all we have to do is what the Lord commanded us to do: "Go ye…" **And then the signs and wonders will follow us!**

Exousia Power

As we read in Luke 10:19, Jesus tells us this: *Behold, I give unto you power to tread on serpents and scorpions, and over all the power of the enemy: and nothing shall by any means hurt you.*

Notice that word *power* **is used twice in this one verse.** The first word *power* is given unto us as believers by the Lord Jesus himself. This word in this verse has a totally different meaning than the word *dynamis* that we previously discussed. This particular word comes from the Greek word *exousia* (ex-oo-see'-ah) **meaning authority, right, privilege, freedom, liberty, or jurisdiction.** The purpose of this type of power is to defeat the Devil (serpents=devils, scorpions=demons). In light of the fact that Jesus defeated the Devil on the cross by snatching from him the keys of death, hell, and the grave and rendering him powerless, we now have received from the Lord Jesus this authority, right, and privilege to use against the Devil as if Jesus himself is using it against him.

Imagine if you will a frail policeman stopping an entire highway flowing with traffic. I'd like you to picture the character Barney Fife from *Mayberry RFD*. He holds his hand out in a stopping motion and demands that they all come to a screeching halt...and they actually stop. How and why? Well, it certainly wasn't because they were afraid of his body build or muscles, and it wasn't even because he looked fierce or intimidating. It was because he was wearing not only a policeman's uniform, but also a badge. That badge represents the city, county, or state in which that policeman has jurisdiction, and if you disrespect that uniform and badge, then you've disrespected the entire city or state he represents, and there will be severe consequences and heavy fines to pay. Thus it is in the spirit realm. This type of power is *exousia*. Satan has to respect the power Jesus has given us over him, regardless. He may not be intimidated by our size or appearance, but when we open our mouths and bind him in Jesus's name, he must respect and obey because he knows he is powerless against us. He sees Christ Jesus in us and is deathly afraid of us because of Jesus. Not only that, he knows our heavenly Father has our backs.

The second word *power*, is the Greek word *dynamis* again, meaning ability and might, referring to Satan's ability and might. So to make it more clear to you, let's re-read this Scripture in Luke 10:19, inserting the Greek words' meanings:*Behold, I give unto you authority, right, privilege, freedom, liberty, and jurisdiction to tread on devils and demons, and over all the ability and might of the enemy: and nothing shall by any means hurt you.*

Hallelujah! With all of this power working on our behalf as believers, how can we not defeat the Devil? How is it that he can stop us from doing the Great Commission? The only one who can stop us from obeying the truth of God's word is the one who looks back at us when we look in the mirror. As Christians, we must put to death the deeds of the flesh.

What Exactly Is My Call Or Purpose In Life?

Here is your exact biblical answer.

Again, God has equipped us to face every single situation that life can throw at us by giving us power—*dynamis* and *exousia*—to handle it head on. So with that in mind, let's read 2 Corinthians 5:17–18:*Therefore if any man be in Christ, he is a new creature: old things are passed away; behold, all things are become new. And all things are of God, who hath reconciled us to himself by Jesus Christ, and hath given to us the ministry of reconciliation.*

God has given every single believer in Christ a mission in life or a ministry, no exceptions. From now on in life, you should not even question what it is that the Lord wants for you to do, because here He has given you the answer as to what you are to do for Him in this life. Your purpose in life or ministry is titled *Ministry of Reconciliation.*

Reconcile means to restore that which was lost, to compose or settle, to bring into proper standing, agreement or harmony. This is what you have been created on this planet to do with your time here on this earth. You are to bring the unsaved world back into right standing with the Father they did not even know they had. You are to do this. This is your assignment and this is a confirmation of God's Great Commission for us as believers. Your job, school, business, and community have become your pulpit from which you are to share the good news of the gospel of Jesus Christ with those you pass by each day. It does not matter what calling or vocation you have in this life, the Lord himself has you positioned here as light in the midst of darkness to be a witness unto Him, whether it be a long-term or short-term job, calling, or vocation. This applies to every single believer alive today, whether we feel worthy or not. This is truly our job on earth until death calls us away or until the Lord returns. Our response should, therefore, be to equip ourselves for such a task in this life.

As you continue reading this book, you will be given the exact tools you need, along with an explanation of how to use these tools for glorious and effective results whereby the Lord would be proud of you. We are the only Jesus this world may ever see. For it is *"Christ in us, the hope of glory!"* (Colossians 1:27).

You Will Be Hated by Society, So Get Used to It!

Now think about that statement for a brief moment, and just let it sink in for a while. Who in his right mind would want to be hated by people of the world in general? No one, I suppose...but wait a minute. Jesus told us we would be hated by the world. Why? Understand that the world lives in spiritual darkness and hates the light of Christianity and understanding. Therefore, we as believers will be hated because *we are the light of the world* (Matthew 5:14). Now if you are not at all hated by the world when Jesus clearly states we will indeed be hated, then ask yourself, "Am I being a light in the midst of darkness, or could I possibly be in the darkness myself? Am I one who does not want to rock the boat? Do I want to be accepted by all peers, saved or not?" This is the place where many Christians live—the in-between place of comfort and political correctness. This was also the place in which the Pharisees of the New Testament lived, a place of neutrality.

God detests neutrality. Revelation 3:16 says, *"So then because thou art lukewarm, and neither cold nor hot, I will spue thee out of my mouth."* We must be willing to go all out for the Lord and His commandment of "Go ye..." or else not go at all. We must make up our minds like Joshua did in Joshua 24:15, *"And if it seems evil unto you to serve the Lord, choose you this day whom ye will serve; whether the gods which your fathers served that were on the other side of the flood, or the gods of the Amorites, in whose land ye dwell: but as for me and my house, we will serve the Lord."*

While this book was being completed in the summer of 2012, one of the main news headlines across America was about attacks against Truett Cathy, founder of Chick-fil-A, for his nonacceptance of same-sex marriage. This man and his sons have devoted most of their lives to pleasing Almighty God and honoring Him by closing all Chick-fil-A restaurants on Sundays to keep the Sabbath Day unto the Lord. He has hired all races, creeds, nationalities, genders, and ages without regard to sexual preferences, across the board. He has given to more charities than you can imagine. But because of his convictions about godly marriage based on the Word of God, many have ostracized him. They have completely shut him out of certain cities, and some mayors have not welcomed the opening of new restaurants in their towns.

As a Christian, if this doesn't make your stomach turn and your blood boil, then you may need to re-examine your walk with Christ. Even our beloved Savior Jesus in Acts 10:38 *"went about doing good, and healing all that were oppressed of the devil, for God was with him."* Jesus only did "good"—not evil, but good—and was still hated by the world. He was not a thief, or a murderer, or an extortioner, nor was he a racist or pedophile, not even a bigot, liar, talebearer, or backbiter, but a good, loving, perfect, forgiving, compassionate man. Yet the world still hates him. Now if our Savior is hated by the world, and the disciple is not greater than his master, what makes you think that the world will love you and me? Below are a few Scripture references where Jesus lets us know that the world will not accept or tolerate us if we do exactly what the Lord tells us to do.

John 15:18–19—*"If the world hate you, ye know that it hated* *me before it hated you. If ye were of the world, the world would love his own: but because ye* are not of the world, but I have chosen you out of the world, therefore the world hateth you."

1 John 3:13—*"Marvel not, my brethren, if the world hate you."*

John 17:14—*"I have given them your word and the world has hated them, for they are not of the world any more than I am of the world"* (NIV).

Matthew 5:11–12—*"Blessed are ye, when men shall revile you, and persecute you, and shall say all manner of evil against you falsely, for my sake. Rejoice, and be exceedingly glad: for great is your reward in heaven: for so persecuted they the prophets which were before you."*

Keep in mind **Matthew 10:24:** *"A disciple is not greater than his master, or a servant than his lord"* (BBE). If they hated Jesus, then they are guaranteed to hate us. Don't sweat it. *"If God be for us, who can be against us?"* (Romans 8:31).

If This Doesn't Convince You, Then Nothing Else Will!

When I say unto the wicked, Thou shalt surely die; and thou givest him not warning, nor speakest to warn the wicked from his wicked way, to save his life; the same wicked man shall die in his iniquity; but his blood will I require at thine hand. (Ezekiel 3:18)

This is pretty much self-explanatory. The Lord obviously is very serious about us doing his will and telling the lost about his ways and his amazing forgiveness of sin. He sends people our way on a regular basis to minister to and to share the love of Christ with. Sometimes the person sent to you as your assignment may not at all be a wonderful or pleasant person. Some may have a filthy, cursing mouth that spews out vulgarities. Others may speak negativity twenty-four hours around the clock because that is how they have been raised. Some hate the mention of God's name, and others are controlled and manipulated by Satan himself. God knew all of this well enough in advance, which is exactly why He equipped us with supernatural (dynamis and exousia) power to get the job done. "How do I do it and what do I say to win them?" Keep on reading this book, because an entire chapter is dedicated to answering that very question.

I'll never forget the testimony I heard on TBN one night. Jeff Fenholt, former lead singer with rock band Black Sabbath shared how he had gotten on a plane to fly to a certain city to perform. Of course, this was after his conversion. Years prior, Jeff had surrendered his heart to Jesus now sings music that glorifies the Lord God.

He was headed to his next city to perform and was extremely lethargic from a long week of ministry. All Jeff wanted was uninterrupted peace and quiet. After all, you really couldn't blame him. He prayed a prayer on that plane as he quietly sat, " Lord, please don't let anyone sit in the seat next to me, and if by chance someone does, please let them not disturb me in any way at all. After all, Lord, I'm really tired. In Jesus's name, Amen." Right before the plane was about to taxi to the runway, a last-minute passenger made his way down the aisle of the plane before the flight attendants closed the door. This young man was a punk rocker all the way, from the holes in the tight jeans to the body piercings, tattoos, and lime-green mohawk hairstyle. He carried his guitar case with him down the aisle looking for his assigned seat. You're probably thinking ahead of me knowing where this is going and you're right. He sat right next to Jeff.

Everything was great for the first few minutes, but when the plane was airborne and the fasten seat belts signs were turned off, this passenger began to ask Jeff about his Bible that lay open on the tray table. "You know, my Grandma used to tell me about the ole good book. If anyone was going to heaven, she was, because she was a good woman. I remember those days, but in all honestly, I've strayed away from it all. One thing led to the next and before you know it, I'm so far away, I wouldn't know how to get back if I wanted to."

Jeff sympathized with the young man, but admitted that he was just too tired to respond and in all honesty wished that the young man would stop talking altogether. Well, his wish came true, the young man fell asleep until the plane landed at its destination. Jeff said good bye to the young rocker, and both of them went their separate ways.

The next day, Jeff ministered to a sold-out audience of people, had an altar call, and many souls came into the kingdom of God that night. Wow, what a successful night, to God be the glory. As Jeff made it back to his hotel room, he opened the door to his room and discovered a newspaper that had been slipped under the door. He picked up the paper and slouched down on his bed to read it. The front-page headline read, "Local rocker found dead in hotel room from overdose of heroine." To Jeff's amazement and unfortunate surprise, the young man was the same young punk rocker who had sat right next to him on the plane. Needless to say, Jeff felt a sickening in his stomach that wouldn't leave him for months.

Let's look again at what the Bible says in response to Jeff's actions. *When I say unto the wicked, Thou shalt surely die; and thou givest him not warning, nor speakest to warn the wicked from his wicked way, to save his life; the same wicked man shall die in his iniquity; but his blood will I require at thine hand.*

How many times has the Lord sent someone to us so we could warn them and share with them the good news of the Lord Jesus? However, because we are often too tied, too busy, ashamed, unprepared, and not discerning of the Lord to know that this person may not be alive within the next day or two, or because we're just too afraid and embarrassed to share the Lord's goodness, we let them die without receiving Jesus. We sometimes convince ourselves that this was their fate regardless; however, God specifically sent them to us for us to minister salvation to without excuse. Eternal damnation—hell—thereby becomes their fate, thanks to us, "the anointed of the Lord!" As stated earlier, we are the hands, feet, and mouthpiece of the Lord and the only Jesus they'll ever see in this life But they died on our watch without any warning at all, and their blood is forever on our hands. **What a travesty!**

God's Great Benefits You Experience as You "Go Ye...!"

- You please the mind and heart of our heavenly Father.
- Soul winning helps develop personal character and integrity in your inner being.
- You save a soul from death and destruction, and God rewards you tremendously.
- Your congregation grows in leaps and bounds, and others in the church are stirred up due to the will of the Lord being fulfilled.
- You are fulfilled and satisfied spiritually, emotionally, and mentally.
- You snatch souls out of hell's fire and defeat the kingdom of darkness.
- Your joy and enthusiasm in the Lord are renewed.
- Your fire is rekindled as you become a threat to the Devil and his kingdom.
- You feel fulfilled because you are operating in your purpose and destiny in life.
- You see the hand of God heal people through your obedience (Mark 16:18).
- Not only will souls thank you down here on Earth for getting them delivered, but many souls in heaven will also thank you for their salvation.

- Creativity is stirred up inside of you. As you do the will of God, other ideas and creativity are stirred up because ideas piggyback off other ideas.
- God's perfect will is carried out according to the Great Commission.
- God can now trust you with other tasks and now uses you in a greater measure.
- Spiritual maturity begins to develop in a profound way.
- God's supernatural wisdom begins to permeate your spirit.
- Your own loved ones are born again and saved due to your obedience in the Lord (Acts 16:31).
- We see the prayers of others' loved ones answered because we choose to "Go ye...!"
- The kingdom of God can now be fulfilled in the earth as we tell the world about our beloved Savior.
- When we lay our heads down to sleep at night, we'll have the sweetest sleep because of the peace of God that will overshadow us.

CHAPTER 9

Bury the Ordinary

You May Not Believe It, but Everyone Is Doing It

Think outside the box. Want better results? Then you must do something totally different. The problem with this world is that many people really don't know who they are and seem to have absolutely no identity. They let the world define them. It is like that picture that is hidden among the confusion and you must stare at it until your eyes eventually focus and see a new, three-dimensional world. That is how it is in the spirit. We are powerful and awesome in the spirit world.

God had Jehoshaphat to put praises on the front line of an active deadly war to praise God. Guess what: it worked. To us, God has a weird sense of humor. He'll make you do something totally out of the ordinary to win souls to the Lord. **News flash:** God hates normal, average, ordinary, mundane, and above all, God hates boredom! The Word of God says in Revelation 3:16, *"So then because thou art lukewarm, and neither cold or hot, I will spue thee out of my mouth."*

Boredom is duplicating soul-winning methods the way every

other church does, such as passing out tracts and witnessing one-on-one, as if that one encounter will automatically change everything in an instant. This is the only method most churches across America use consistently. Think about this and let it sink in for a moment. Is this all the church has to offer to the world when it comes to our trying to reach the masses for the kingdom of God? Witnessing tracts, is that it? Boring, dead, dry witnessing tracts with a lot of writing on them? Would you read all of that if you were not a Christian?

God hates normal, average, ordinary, mundane, and boring. Average is to be the best of the worst and to be the worst of the best. Average is to be the top of the bottom and the bottom of the top. To the Lord, this is simply boring.

God has new methods of winning a new generation to Himself compared to previous years. He hasn't changed His message, but He has changed the methods by which we do things. *"Where sin abounds, grace much more abounds"* (Romans 5:20). It is sad to say, but unfortunately, the church can actually learn a thing or two from the world. The world is living a lie in a grand, celebratory way that attracts people like flies, whereas the church is living the absolute truth in a raggedy, shabby way that repels people. However, change is taking place for the body of Christ, because we're going out in a full blaze of glory, taking the world with us into the kingdom of God in heaven, hallelujah!

All God Needs Is a Remnant of Obedient People to Get the Job Done.

Satan, the archenemy of God, is not at all bothered by churches that are noneffective and have merely settled down to a social-club status. Satan is not even bothered with large numbers in congregations. But he is concerned about an active, volcanic, proportionate, supercharged church doing the will of God: a "Go ye…" church. A congregation operating in their optimum prime is more of a triple threat to the Devil than you can imagine, no matter how large or small the congregation itself might be.

Massive numbers are not what really moves God, either, but obedient people move the hands of our God. "But I don't feel led!" Many people worldwide use this statement as an excuse. **Well, get the lead out of your britches and get out there and move for the Lord!** There are many things the Lord has asked us to do, yet at times we may not feel that we are in the position to do the will of God, or we don't feel led. However, we must still obey the Lord. It is not based on a feeling, but on obedience and doing what we know to do at the right time.

When the Lord can get a few in a church to obey his every command, then the masses will come out as a result of the "Go ye…!" church. God only needs a remnant of obedient servants to do his will, and the multitudes of souls are the results of obedience. It took only twelve disciples to turn the world upside down for Jesus. Peter singlehandedly preached a message and three thousand souls were saved. On another occasion when Peter preached, five thousand souls were saved. God called Gideon and told him he had too many soldiers to fight with, even though they were severely outnumbered. He went from thirty-two thousand soldiers to only three hundred. It took only three hundred soldiers to defeat the Midianites, with the help of the Lord.

So don't get discouraged if you only have a few volunteers to sign up for street witnessing or evangelism for the week, because God can do wonders with just a few; I've seen it in my own life time after time. So let's buckle up for an exciting ride that will stretch your faith and take you to an absolutely new dimension of church growth according to the Word of God.

Again, I must warn you that if these principles are applied, your church will never be in the same shape as it was before, but it will be stretched to another level, which may cause spiritual stretch marks denoting exponential growth. Jesus commands us to "Go ye therefore into all the world and preach the gospel." Remember, this is indeed a command and not an option. When we simply do through obedience what the Lord has commanded us to do, we will see the same results that the apostles saw in the book of Acts without fail.

Let's Learn a Lesson or Two from Secular Society

One of my all-time favorite entertainers was Michael Jackson. I know what you're thinking: "Michael Jackson was not even a Christian. In fact, he was into all kinds of messed-up stuff." How true you are, and whether he went to heaven or hell, only God knows because I certainly would not want to be the one on the seat of judgment to say where his soul went. Again, only the Lord knows. However, my point is this; that man electrified his audiences every single time he performed. One could not sit still at one of his concerts, whether live or video, and be bored, even if someone paid you to be. He had sensationalism to attract everyone in the audience. He had a way of making you literally sit on the edge of your seat with amazement and anticipation for his next step or song.

Although I am not at all a fan of Lady Gaga, she too has the same type of captivating power to overwhelm her audiences because she lives on the edge of wildness, freakiness, and controversy. What exactly am I trying to convey to you with such explicit examples? I'm so glad you asked.

This is my point: the secular world captivates and glamorizes audiences in such a way that even two- and three-year-olds are popping their fingers to the beat of nonproductive rhetoric that attracts and captivates them. But when it comes to the church trying to reach this same world captivated by sensationalism, the only thing we offer this unsaved generation after a command of the Lord to "Go ye" is a gospel tract and a prayer. What a joke! How can we compete with the Devil with such predictable tactics? Satan knows this; that is why to the Devil, some of us Christians are indeed a joke, and he does not even try to stop us because he knows that we are spinning our wheels getting absolutely nowhere.

To us as believers, it appears to be a "good work." However, good works are not at all necessarily "God works." God works are ordained by the Lord through the Holy Spirit, whereas good works are done as a result of habit or teaching that we've been accustomed to doing without necessarily being led by the Holy Spirit.

Listen, when the Holy Spirit steps in and does a work, all hell breaks out in convulsions and sweat; Satan is furious and goes ballistic because he knows that there is absolutely nothing he can do to stop it and results are inevitable. We must keep in mind that when it comes to winning souls into the kingdom of God, He is with us in every step because these are His people and He is concerned about them more than you and I will ever know. So as we are yielded to His Holy Spirit, He will give us witty techniques and use us in creative ways and in unusual settings.

Breaking out of the ordinary includes using all creative means and mechanisms that God gave us to make our presentation to the world an exciting experience. The anointing of the Lord upon us is sensationalism. In fact, it far surpasses sensationalism. Unlike Michael Jackson or Lady Gaga, it does not just look good or sound good, but the Holy Spirit's sensationalism makes you walk, talk, and do good. How then can we captivate an audience to the point where they will listen to what we have to say and hang on the edge of their seats?

Ever heard of miracles, signs, and wonders? These tactics never fail. In fact, Michael Jackson, Lady Gaga, and whoever might be to you a sensational entertainer, sports hero, or idol, cannot compare to God's power in action. Even these great electrifying entertainers would be considered extremely boring next to God's power in full action. Seem too far-fetched? Have you ever read Mark 16:15–20?

> *And he said unto them, "Go ye into all the world, and preach the gospel to every creature. He that believeth and is baptized shall be saved; but he that believeth not shall be damned. And these signs shall follow them that believe; In my name shall they cast out devils; they shall speak with new tongues; They shall take up serpents; and if they drink any deadly thing, it shall not hurt them; they shall lay hands on the sick, and they shall recover. So then after the Lord had spoken unto them, he was received up into heaven, and sat on the right hand of God. And they went forth, and preached every where, the Lord working with them, and confirming the word with signs following. Amen.*

We've talked a little about this in a previous chapter, but bear with me. This point deserves repeating with a new twist. Notice that "these signs shall follow them that believe," not "them that believe shall follow these signs." If you are a believer, then these signs will follow you as you "Go ye...!" This is for real; no joke or hype. If you believe God's word, these signs will actually follow you if you simply put God to the test. Also notice in verse 20 that "they went forth and preached every where."

After they obeyed the Lord and went forth doing the Great Commission by preaching or witnessing to nonbelievers, notice that the Lord was working with them. How comforting to know that when we just simply do the command of "Go ye," Jesus will inevitably be with us every single step of the way working with us and confirming His word with signs following.

Please pay close attention to the order of God in the context of this particular Scripture. I say this because many believers want to see the power of God in action in their church or on the streets just like they did in the Bible days. Many followed Jesus only for the loaves and the fishes or the signs and wonders. This is what God wants to do for his church and the body of Christ at large, that is, to show Himself strong.

However, if we simply obey the Lord's command and his Great Commission, we will see miracles, signs and wonders follow us like the wind. As we share the gospel of Jesus through obedience, the Lord will confirm his word. What word? His words that are spoken through us as we tell someone about the goodness of the Lord through witnessing; that word! The "Go ye…" word! After we obey and become witnesses, great things will happen to us because God will confirm everything that we just bragged about Him through signs that will follow.

God Will Do Demonstrations of His Spirit among the Crowds

I'll never forget the time we were preaching the gospel over the speaker system in an impoverished community full of drugs and violence. As I stood up to preach with a microphone in my hand, a couple of kids were riding their bicycles quite fast down a really steep hill. One little boy lost control, fell hard and violently onto the concrete, and did not move after he had fallen. All one could hear were loud screams as nearly everyone around that area ran to see the fate of this young child. Not to sound selfish, but in my mind, this could have not happened at a worse time. I seemed to have captivated the crowd's attention because of the anointing of the Lord working through me, and I thought of all the souls who might have given their hearts to the Lord when I gave the altar call. Instead, their attention was diverted to the child. At this point, I was indeed concerned about that little boy and even asked the Lord what to do. I clearly heard the Lord say to me to lay my hands on the young child and to pray for him, so I hastily did just that. I had to press my way through screaming people, including the little boy's mother.

As I approached the child lying on the dirty concrete ground, the little boy appeared to be unconscious so I just leaned over, laid my hand upon him and prayed, "Lord God in heaven, show your strong hand here today by raising this child up right now among this crowd of people without any broken bones or injuries at all in Jesus name, amen!" Immediately the child rose up, brushed himself off, and got right back on his bicycle as if nothing at all had ever happened. He did not even shed a tear. Wow! Talking about a modern-day miracle! Jesus simply kept his end of the deal. The Lord was working with me confirming His word with signs following. I'm sure you can imagine how the rest of the evening went. That evening, 120 people gave their hearts to the Lord at the altar. Satan lost another round by trying to distract, yet the Lord had a greater plan.

Another Black Eye Given to the Devil!

I can recall an instance when I sat at my home office desk just bored out of my wits. It was an extremely beautiful spring day, and the sun was out, but I was just restless not knowing completely what the Lord had in store for my life. Have you ever felt like that? This was not at all a good feeling, but a feeling of uselessness. With my head slumped down on my desk, I felt like a failure. I may have done a million and one things for the kingdom of God up to that point, but in my mind, I hadn't done hardly anything or nearly enough for Jesus.

During these times, we are more vulnerable to Satan than any other times, and if we are not careful, the Devil can whisper negative voices into our minds that can change the entire course of our destinies. These are moments of warfare in which we must engage with the Devil if we plan to win. We must do what King David did; that is, to encourage ourselves in the Lord. Rather than feeling sorry for myself or having self-pity, I decided to give the Devil another black eye at that moment by praising God with all of my might. So the next thing I did was telephone a fiery Christian companion of mine named Melvin.

I decided to go to one of the worst areas in all of downtown Atlanta, known as Kirkwood, on one of the worst streets of that area, where many drug dealers hung out selling their product. Melvin was right there with me. We were both completely prayed up and were eagerly waiting the instructions of the Lord concerning our marching orders. Melvin asked me in a confident voice, "Was this on your agenda, or did you just come up with this?"

I had to admit, "I was just bored and wanted to beat the Devil down because I was allowing him to get the best of me, so if the Devil wants to play hardball, hardball it is!" So with Holy Ghost boldness, we approached over twenty-eight drug dealers on top of a hill, along with their scantily dressed girlfriends. All were waiting for the next drug customers to drive up in their cars to make the exchange for their illegal hustle. Many of them had guns underneath their shirts. With boldness like lions, Melvin and I approached this entire group, and the Holy Spirit was so strong upon us that we almost gloated as we approached them. "Who's in charge here?" I asked with Holy Ghost authority.

Several guys surrounded us and asked if we were five-0—police. "No, we're not five-0, I just noticed you're selling that weak stuff, and we've got something more powerful than you can ever imagine that will put that stuff to a total shame."

"What you got?" one guy asked. "His name is Jesus!" I responded. It was as if a bomb had exploded when I said Jesus' name. Many expletives were used to say the least, and one guy yelled out, "Lord have mercy."

Melvin and I boldly witnessed to that entire group of about twenty-eight young men, along with eighteen women, and sixteen of the men surrendered their hearts to the Lord alone, with about ten women. They bowed down on their knees in the dirt with hands lifted toward heaven and asked Jesus Christ to come into their lives as if this were a drug bust or something. I kid you not, genuine tears flowed down in streams from many of their eyes as they on one accord repeated the sinners' prayer by asking our beloved Savior to enter into their hearts. What a day of rejoicing that was for Melvin and me! Just think, to go into the enemy's camp and boldly snatch out twenty-six souls from the kingdom of darkness into the kingdom of God. Hallelujah!

At the end of the day, back in my office, I asked the Lord why it was that he wouldn't use me like that every day of my life. God's response was amazing to me. The Lord told me so clearly, "Charles, I would take delight in using you like this every day of your life if you would only yield to me daily like you did today. Today you went forth doing my command, and I was there with you just as I promised. I will be there with you always confirming my word with signs following. *Your heart prepares your way, but I direct your path.* (Proverbs 16:9)

It's Amazing How Fire Will Attract

The great John Wesley said, "I set myself on fire, and people come out to watch me burn." If you want to see the greatness of God in your ministry, your life, in your church, your community, and even in the world, you must indeed bury the ordinary and think outside of the entire box. With the Lord on our side, the sky is literally the limit.

In closing this chapter, I'd like to share a true story that happened to us at a church we attended in a nice community. My wife and I had attended this particular church for almost seven years. This is the same church I mentioned in the chapter titled "Wrong Pastor for the Right Job."

I had just developed an evangelism program there that was extremely successful, but very abruptly the pastor pulled the plug on the program and shut us down. I tried to be very respectful to the pastor because after all, it was his vision that I submitted myself under. I asked him respectfully if he would tell me why we had to shut down a successful evangelistic ministry indefinitely. His response was because he felt that the Lord was leading him in another direction. During this time, many people were beginning to leave because he had begun to preach like a dictator.

We stayed there faithfully for three more long years, until the Lord gave us a release to leave in an orderly way. While waiting it out for those remaining three years, I remember one of those years the church literally catching on fire. The fire could be seen for miles because the church was engulfed and totally consumed with fire. It seemed the entire community of about three hundred people came out to watch that church burn on a clear, hot, spring afternoon.

As many members of the church stood outside among the larger crowd of people to watch the entire church burn up, the pastor loudly asked, "My God, where did all these people come from?"

Someone yelled out "They've been here all along!"

Then the pastor said, "Well, I've never seen this many before!"

Then someone else yelled out louder, **"Well this church has never been on fire before either."**

Wow, let that sink in a minute. Just something to think about.

CHAPTER 10

Attention Getters: God's Bait

I was recently invited as a guest on a local cable TV channel to discuss evangelism as a whole. The host asked me to explain how I got started with the street services that have lasted for more than thirty years. In response, I told him that for the first eleven years, we struggled with trying to get the masses of people to come out to those street services. Now keep in mind, at sixteen years of age, after accepting the Lord into my heart, I started by ministering to one or two individuals at a time and would be successful in winning their souls to Christ. This eventually became an obsession with me to the point that I felt the entire world's fate lay upon my shoulders and that I needed to share Christ with the world. So instead of witnessing to one or two individuals, I would minister to dozens of people per day in hopes of winning at least five to ten people to the Lord. This went on for at least a year and a half. I felt a strong need in my heart to win the masses to Christ.

During the street services, we would set up the sound equipment, have singing, preaching, and even praise dancing, but this would only be for a crowd of at least twenty or thirty people. Now some of you might feel as if that might have been a nice-size crowd of people to minister to, but this size in reference to the size of the community at large was not nearly enough. Several communities we ministered to had over five hundred residents with only a small percentage attending those street services. How then do I reach the masses? This was the prevailing question in my mind that I would constantly struggle with in my prayers to the Lord.

I can recall one particular community in Atlanta called Capital Homes, where my eyes opened in a eureka moment that would forever change the direction and the results of the street services from that point forward.

Before this moment, I had gotten so frustrated I questioned whether I was even in God's will or not. I would ask Him, "Lord, how can we get the attention of these people to come out and support what we are trying to do in Your name?" The only reply I received from the Lord was a still, soft voice speaking back to me within my heart saying, *"He that winneth souls is wise"* (Proverbs 11:30). Think about that for just a second; it was as if the Lord Himself were actually taking the ball and throwing it back to me in my corner. What was I supposed to do with that type of a response?

As I paced the street sidewalk back and forth in deep deep thought, this eureka moment occurred as if a light bulb had been turned on in my mind: *money!* What person in his right mind would turn down money? As easy as it may sound, now a bigger problem presented itself: Where do I get money to pass out? Now, what I'm about to tell you, I would never recommend to anyone ever under any circumstances; however, this is exactly what I did, but only this one time. The great thing about our God is that He still watches over us even in our ignorance. This will make a little more sense as you continue to read.

This is what came to my mind. There are gospel witnessing tracts that look identical to U.S. twenty-dollar bills. You may have seen them before. There is the face of President Thomas Jefferson on the front, which looks almost identical to a regular twenty-dollar bill, but on the back of this gospel tract is written the plan of salvation. Honestly, you could almost be deceived by someone because of the realness of how it looks.

We bought a pack of these gospel tracts that looked like twenty-dollar bills and headed to Capital Homes in downtown Atlanta. Our agenda was to knock on every door in the community and tell everyone there that we are passing out twenty-dollar bills to all who show up for the street meeting. **Word to the wise, never pass out any food, clothing, toys, etc. until you have had your meeting first,** or else everyone will leave as soon as they get what you have to offer, because they only want what you have to offer, not necessarily the gospel of Jesus. To our amazement, over 350 people showed up in that small housing project community. How do I know this? Because we brought with us 315 chairs, and all were filled up with many others standing around. After I preached the gospel and gave an altar call, approximately 135 people gave their hearts to the Lord.

Now before the altar call, we made it extremely clear that everyone would receive a twenty-dollar bill for coming, whether they stood up to accept the Lord or not, so this proved that their choice for the Lord was, in fact, genuine. After all the dust settled and everyone returned to their seats, our team passed out the twenty-dollar bill gospel tracts. Of course it only took a second before everyone present knew it was a fake, but in my defense, I said over the loudspeakers, "I told you all that if you showed up you would receive a twenty-dollar bill. Well, you did receive a twenty-dollar bill; I never told you it would be a real one."

Needless to say, some people were cursing mad, while others laughed it off as fun. However, I never did that again because something like that could actually turn out dangerous or even deadly. That is why I thank God that He watched over us in our ignorance during those early days. Eventually, our church would go on to collect offerings for our street services, and then advertise that there would be cash given away afterwards. This was done by way of asking the audience a biblical question, and by the show of hands if that particular person gave the right answer, we would give him a real ten- or twenty-dollar bill. This approach won us much favor in many communities without any incidents or threats.

After I shared all of this with the host of this local cable TV station, in response he said, "You know, it surely is a shame that the body of Christ has to stoop to such a level of desperation to lure people to hear the gospel message rather than just preaching the uncompromising raw gospel of Jesus." At that point, he shook my hand and ended the interview without even giving me the chance to respond. The way the host ended the interview almost made me sound like a villain. So now you have the pleasure of getting my response to that interview.

The question that comes to mind is, why is it that ministries sometimes use bait or attention getters to reach people? To many believers, this sounds a bit like a gimmick. Why then do we do it? Jesus did not use baits to get people to follow Him... or did He?

Look at it this way. Jesus preached the raw gospel message that hit people so hard in between the eyes that one of two things took place: either a revival broke out, or a riot broke out. At one point, Jesus had to run ahead of the crowds before the self-righteous religious leaders tried to cast Him over a cliff (Luke 4:28–29). But how and why did people follow a man from Galilee whom they had never seen before? Well, they may not have actually seen Him before, but they had indeed heard of Him because of His reputation and the fact that He performed many miracles, which preceded Him. **You could say that Jesus' bait was the miracles, signs, and wonders he performed.** God used this as bait to draw the crowds of people. In fact, at one time so many people followed Jesus that He discerned many followed for the wrong reasons: the loaves and the fishes and the signs (John 6:26–27). We can further corroborate this story with Scripture from Acts 2, where the Lord used the gift of speaking in tongues as bait to attract over three thousand souls. These people were overwhelmed and impressed by the fact that unlearned Jews spoke in their language more fluently than they themselves. That day after Peter preached, three thousand souls were saved and added to the kingdom.

Notice that the Devil uses bait to blind the minds of individuals who don't believe the gospel of Christ. No one seems to mind that idea. Keep in mind, the Devil will never be able to outdo our Lord in any way.

Have you ever noticed that if there is an advertisement for a revival in town, many times you'll hear about it on the radio or television and you'll usually hear somewhere in the advertisement about healing the sick, or prophetic conference, or maybe a big-name Christian artist? Well, these are all baits that are used to draw people out to that church or facility. Why bait or use attention getters? Simple—the world loves darkness over light, so what makes you think that nonbelievers will just break down the church doors to get in versus going to a secular event that will fulfill their lust and appease their ungodly desires? How then do we get sinners to come to church? We intercede for them in prayer that God will shake up their world to bring them to a state of repentance, and then we as believers go out to them and win them to the Lord.

Mike Murdock said, "If you want something that you've never had, you've got to do something that you've never done, because if you keep on doing what you've always done, then you'll keep on getting what you've always gotten." While some ministers are content to have average results and have the same mind-set as the host of that cable TV show, others want to see exponential results and outstanding moves of God in our world after we take the limits off of God. *"The people who know their God shall be strong, and carry out great exploits"* (Daniel 11:32, NKJV).

Remember: *"Go ye into all the world and preach the gospel..."*

The Bible also states that *"the harvest is ripe, but the laborers are few, pray therefore that the Lord of the harvest would send forth more laborers into the vineyard"* (Matthew 9:37). We pray for the unsaved as if it all depends on God, but we actually go after them with wisdom to win them to Christ as if it all depends on us. Here are a handful of ideas and wisdom nuggets that your church can use as bait to bring in a harvest of souls for the kingdom of our Lord.

Dinner and a Play

Our church evangelism ministry passed out ten thousand flyers and invited people to come out to our church during Thanksgiving 2009. The flyers read, "The first 1,800 families to come out to our church will receive three boxes of groceries and one turkey per family." We had teamed up with the Feed the Hungry ministry to make all of this possible. We also made the mistake of announcing this event over the air on one of the most popular Christian radio stations in the city of Atlanta. So many people showed up, the lines were wrapped around the building even an hour and a half before the program began. We had well over 6,000 people show up, and our sanctuary only seats 4,500. We had to put an additional 2,000-plus seats in the overflow section of the Fellowship Hall.

You're probably thinking, well that is a con to get people to come out to your church. Well, is anything wrong with this bait? Was dishonesty used in any way? Remember the word of the Lord, *"He that winneth souls is wise"* (Proverbs 11:29). We also performed a play that same night titled *The Judgment*, which consisted of pyrotechnics—fire, sparks, and loud cannon sounds—during the "hell" scene. When all was done, there were so many souls raising their hands for salvation, until there was no room to come down to the altar. We just had them recite the sinner's prayer of salvation right there where they were standing. There were, conservatively, about 2,500–3,000 souls who stood up to receive Jesus Christ into their hearts that evening. This number does not even include the ones located in the overflow section. Say or believe what you wish, but if we had not offered the free food and done the radio announcement, without a doubt, probably less than half that number of people, or even a smaller fraction, would have shown up that night. Of course, your budget may not allow for ten thousand flyers, not to mention 1,800 boxes of groceries and turkeys, but whatever you have, let it be a blessing and bait used to bring your community into your church for you to introduce them to Christ.

Neighborhood Gymnasium

One of my new pastor friends, Pastor Neil Bernard, who founded the New Wine Christian Fellowship Church in Laplace, Louisiana, devised a brilliant idea for bait. He renovated an entire plaza and made one part his church, another part his kitchen, and other parts were turned into office spaces. I was really impressed with the fact that he turned an old Kmart store into a gymnasium. One would think, "Wow, it surely takes a ton of money to get a project like that off the ground." But remember one thing: our boss Jesus will indeed provide the resources if we simply come up with the vision.

Pastor Bernard has a powerful testimony behind this story that will send chills up and down your spine. Sight is a function of the eyes, but vision is a function of the heart. What moves the hand of God in our lives as believers is vision; without it, the people perish or cast off restraints (Proverbs 29:18). If any pastor has a vision that is attainable and makes sense, God will see to it that his vision takes off as he yields himself to God through prayer. After all, it was the Lord who placed that vision in the heart of the pastor in the first place, so he could pray the will of God that was in his heart back to the Father in heaven. *"If we ask any thing according to His will, He heareth us"* (1 John 5:14). If you and I can personally finance the vision we have in our hearts for God's kingdom to be done here on earth as it is in heaven, then that vision is probably not from the Lord. God will always give us a vision so, so big it could only be financed by Him. And nine times out of ten, it will outlast us, and other generations after us will have to continue it.

Pastor Bernard received a miracle from the Lord when it came to his renovating this Kmart into a gymnasium. Directly behind his church is a minimum-security prison that is so close to the back of his church one could literally throw a rock at it. A barbed-wire fence separates the prison from the church at the former Kmart center. Pastor Bernard had been visiting and ministering there at the prison for years, telling the prisoners about the goodness of our Savior Jesus. He would always bring a team of his faithful members with him to reach the lost souls in that prison. God touched the prison warden's heart and gave Pastor Bernard miraculous favor. The warden created a schedule, as part of the prisoners' curriculum, for them to help Pastor Bernard renovate the Kmart into a gymnasium absolutely free of charge, until the entire project was completely finished. All Pastor Bernard had to do was feed them daily and nothing else. Now that sounds like one of the miracles one reads directly out of the Bible. Up to this very day, many young souls pack this gymnasium, and a large percentage of these souls have committed their hearts to the Lord Jesus and actually attend Pastor Bernard's church.

Needless to say, the ones who have served their time in prison and are released become not only members of his church but also very productive citizens who impact their community in a positive way. This is what I call **"desperate measures of explosive church growth."**

Cruise with a Cause

Matthew Dunaway, an ordinary layman (no doubt, not for long) from Alabama and a very good friend of mine came up with a crazy, out-of-this-world idea that not too many people would even have the faith to imagine: Charter an entire cruise ship, fill it up with Christians with hearts of evangelism wanting to fulfill the "Go ye..." command, do away with the gambling and cocktail drinks and minister to an entire island for Jesus. This kind of crazy, weird thinking birthed Praisefest Ministries' "Cruise with a Cause" founded by Matthew Dunaway.

Talking about an attention getter—who would say no to an extremely affordable cruise? And not just any cruise. Matthew assembled a team of strong Christian believers about five years ago to form his board of directors, of which I can proudly yet graciously say I am a member. He then set his sights on reaching the islands of the Bahamas, Jamaica, Haiti, and many others that are waiting the Lord's timing and approval. Now imagine this: You fill up an entire cruise ship with Christians and invite some of America's top preachers, Christian song artists, and Christian comedians for ministry. Not only are all of the believers on the ship serenaded with preaching, teaching, singing, and laughter, but also the island is bombarded by believers who will introduce them to our wonderful Lord and Master, Jesus Christ. Matthew has it structured in a way that fulfills the Lord's Great Commission to the fullest.

On the ship, every believer is given simple instructions. He may choose one of three different avenues of ministry in which to participate while on the island. One third of the group ministers to all of the prisons on that island within a certain proximity, another third ministers to all of the elementary and high school students, and the last third ministers on the streets with the loudspeaker in different parts of the island. This pretty much covers all bases. A stadium-type location is booked for the ultimate concert experience. This concert is free of charge. While the entire group breaks out into three segments, the invitation to the concert is given to all participants that day for them to return later that evening with their family members and friends. The concert is a collaboration of all the Christian song artists, performing to an audience of twenty thousand souls or more, and at the end an altar call is given.

We have seen tens of thousands of souls give their hearts unto the Lord right there on the spot, not to mention the souls who were saved earlier in the schools, prisons, and on the streets. You may ask again, how was he able to amass such a large sum of money to make all of this come to pass? For the first three years, God touched the heart of a multimillionaire who was moved by Matthew's awesome vision. He was able to finance about 80 percent of the budget of this megaventure for Matthew. Where there is a megavision, God always has provisions for the vision. Remember, the Master's heart is for us to "Go ye…!" As we prepare to go without any questions asked, He does the rest.

Tribulation Trail

A Stockbridge, Georgia, church annually holds an outdoor drama based on the Bible's book of Revelation. It's called *Tribulation Trail.* This wonderful bait, if you will, draws more than 16,000 visitors. The church holds the event annually, each Friday and Saturday evening during the month of October. Reports are that about 1,600 confirmed salvations take place during that month due to the presentation, not to mention about 5,000 or more re-dedications to the Lord.

Tribulation Trail begins with a conversation among God, Jesus, and the Holy Spirit about God's concern with fallen mankind and his plan to redeem man. It continues by depicting twelve scenes from the Bible, and concludes with the "River of Life," the depiction of God's plan, in which humans are invited into eternal life. This is all done in the backyard of the church on many acres that takes one on a literal trail. It takes about forty-five to sixty minutes to walk through all the scene setups on the trail. Afterward, counselors from the church meet with visitors to discuss their relationship with God and at that point lead them in the sinner's prayer.

Preparations for *Tribulation Trail* involve supervising parking, providing security, setting up lighting, operating the concession stand and ticket booth, as well as special effects. It takes about three hundred people to put it on. Maybe your church's entire congregation is less than three hundred people. Then you could use what you have and do something similar to this event on a smaller scale and still see large results.

Sweep Team

Many years ago when I attended high school, we were required to take R.O.T.C. whether we wanted to or not. I tried out for the Color Guard, and to my amazement, I was chosen. The Color Guard consisted of four soldiers who carried or escorted the flags, or colors, during ceremonies or parades, reviews, etc. After many years, the Lord brought the idea of the Color Guard back to my mind. So I devised a military-style team of individuals that I called The SWEEP Team. SWEEP is an acronym for Soul Winning Evangelistically Energized Posse. This team originally consisted of about forty-four people both male and female, but dwindled down to about twenty-four consistent people. Custom military-style costumes or uniforms were, made similar to the Color Guard uniforms that the Lord gave me in a vivid vision. Fake wooden rifles were purchased and used in our routine drills. Drills were learned and performed pretty much like any army drill team but with a jazzy twist. Much time and practice were devoted to perfecting the steps and routines. I must admit we were pretty sharp in our dress, drill routines, and the way we delivered our presentation.

Looking back today, we could have easily been contestants on *America's Got Talent* and probably would have won, or at least been in second place. People would stop and drop what they were doing to sit, stand, or just drive by to watch us do our thing. After large crowds would gather around, we did a routine of cadence magnifying the Lord Jesus.

I would shout out in question "Who are you?"

Their response in unison would be, "We are the Word of Faith SWEEP Team, sir!"

"And what is the Word of Faith SWEEP Team?"

"Soul Winning Evangelistically Energized Posse, sir!"

"And what do you sweep?"

"We sweep up Satan's mess so that people who come to know Christ can be blessed, sir!"

"And how do you sweep up Satan's mess?"

"By violently snatching souls from darkness into the kingdom of light, sir!"

This performance of drills and different cadences went on for about fifteen to twenty minutes. Afterward, each member would "fall out" and mingle with the crowds by way of one-on-one witnessing and by passing out Chick tracts about the Lord, and we would pray for individuals who needed prayer. Inevitably many souls were saved and added to God's kingdom by way of the prayer of salvation in every one of our performances. This went on for about six years before we finally disbanded for good due to individual team members getting married, having children, going back to school, and so on.

PIN

Another friend of mine who is a fiery evangelist came up with an unusual way of attracting many crowds of people for the gathering of the gospel message. This unusual method was derived by the Holy Spirit and given to my friend Curtis Minter along with his wife, Bobbie. PIN is an acronym for Power In Names. God has blessed this couple with a prophetic gift that enables them to tell the individual they are ministering to about themselves based on his or her full name being written on a piece of paper, or on a chalkboard or whiteboard supported by an easel. They will set up a whiteboard at practically any location—cruise ships, church vestibules, small parties, home gatherings, and many other locations. It is a God-given gift that allows them to speak into the lives of people with precision and accuracy simply based on that person writing his full name on this whiteboard. I have personally seen many lives changed by a prophetic word that they have received based on this gift of God in operation. I guess you could call it the word of knowledge channeled through the person's name. Once this gift is in motion, the lines are packed with people anxiously waiting for an opportunity to receive a prophetic word based on their name. You know that God is in control, because this couple does this without any charge, but donations are welcomed. What an excellent bait to lead many souls into the Kingdom of God by encouragement through **Power In Names.**

Exodus

One local Christian radio DJ, a personal friend of mine who is extremely well known in the Atlanta area and surrounding suburbs, devised a mega way of attracting countless unsaved youth. He used his influence that God has given him by way of radio. Corey Condrey, founder of The Condrey Evangelistic Association, periodically hosts a major production called *Exodus*, to which he invites Christian artists along with well-known secular artists and has a major celebration for Jesus. The last one took place in October 2012 at the Condrey Retreat west of Atlanta. Now, I know what some religious minds are thinking right about now about having secular artists participate in a Christian production, but remember the Word of God, "He that winneth souls is wise."

The secular artists are a drawing card or bait to bringing out the unsaved. They are asked to put on a clean show: no profanity, no seductive acts of any sort. Then afterward, Christian artists are brought out to perform as well. A powerful minister delivers the word of God in a practical way, then an altar call is given as thousands are saved in an instant. In December 2011, over 38,000 people attended the Georgia Dome, and over 2000 plus souls were saved during the altar call, and over 1,500 were baptized that same night. This is an excellent way to use your influence if you are high-profile.

Street Service During Secular Event

Several years ago, Atlanta experienced three or four consecutive years of college campus breaks called "Freaknic." This was the gathering of many local African American universities as well as out-of-state universities. The students would just hang out at many club spots and local parks to do nothing but party. The only problem with this was that so many students, as well as non students, would show up and crowd the city of Atlanta and traffic became a nightmare. This would last for an entire weekend in the spring, usually during April or May, and though it brought plenty of money to many Atlanta businesses, things would oftentimes get terribly out of control.

To counteract the destructive ways that Satan swayed people, our church came up with a brilliant strategy to win souls to Christ during these times of reveling and wild behavior. We set up our sound system with six powerful speakers, a stage, singers, Christian rappers, and praise dancers and really gave the crowds something to celebrate, that is, our beloved Savior Jesus!

I can clearly recall one year when things at Freaknic got so badly out of hand that some young girls were even raped, and this was the talk on most local news channels. So because of the boldness and the obedience that the Lord God graced us to have, our church set up the stage right in the middle of all of the commotion.

As we prepared to minister to the crowds, out of nowhere appeared a young girl wearing a skimpy bikini and riding on a horse in the midst of this large crowd. All of the young college-age men were pulling her off the horse and fondling her body. She rode the horse into a gas station on a corner and the young guys tried to have their way with her sexually right there during the daylight hours. The next thing I'm about to describe to you was nothing short of a miracle of God Almighty.

A very good pastor friend of mine by the name of Dr. Reginald Garmon, who was with our group, stood up on a trash can underneath the gas station awning in the midst of about one hundred and fifty to two hundred men (not counting any women) that were trying to grope this young girl, who was obviously void of understanding. As he stood up on that trash can without a microphone or sound system—which were across the street along with the stage setup—the power of God hit him in such a way that I would equate this to a modern-day miracle. Such a boldness came from his mouth as he yelled at the top of his lungs "Leave that young girl alone now! That's somebody's daughter you are messing with; I rebuke this behavior in the name of Jesus!" Believe it or not, these hundreds of young guys stopped dead in their tracks and walked away from that unwise young girl. She stood there shaking and fearing for her very life. It was as if God amplified Reverend Garmon's voice louder than a sound system, and the fear of Almighty God came on each one of those young men and they could not do any harm to that young girl, so they hastily walked away.

We had the best street service the rest of that day, and many souls were brought into the kingdom of God despite what dysfunctional plans the Devil may have had for the crowd of people. The ironic thing about this whole story is that on that very corner where the gas station is still located, Reverend Garmon has a large billboard sign there advertising the location of his church, Word of Faith Love Center, which is only a mile or so away from that very spot. It's as if God Almighty placed a memorial or a marker at that spot to remind Reverend Garmon where the power was first magnified in his ministry life.

Other Witty Ways of Attracting Crowds as Bait for Ministry

Offer members an incentive. A pastor friend once used a 42-inch flat-screen LED TV as an incentive to get his entire congregation to invite many unsaved as well as saved individuals to his church. His congregation size was about 350 people. The first person or family that invited fifteen or more people would win the flat-screen TV. Because of this incentive, there were seventy-eight people invited to his church that month alone. He was also generous enough to give a second-place prize as well. Once the people respond and attend your church, it is up to a prepared pastor and the Holy Spirit to keep them there.

Sidewalk Sunday school. Your ministry or church could go to neighborhoods in your community to set up fun things to do for the kids in the neighborhood and invite them and their parents to attend your church service.

Neighborhood boil. I had never in my life heard of such a thing until a busload of us went to New Orleans during the aftermath of Hurricane Katrina. We worshiped with a church there that had a boil. This was an event where the church invited the neighborhood to come out and eat with them as they ate crab legs, shrimp, and other foods that are boiled.

Outside play. At this same boil, we performed an outside play for the crowds to gather and come out to watch. This was really going outside the box. Many individuals showed up for this event, many tears were shed, and several souls were saved that evening. We put quite a bit of money into the costumes to make sure we would have a greater impact on the people that showed up. It was a brief play depicting the Lord Jesus's crucifixion, which indeed paid off by way of multiple souls surrendering their hearts to the Lord that very night.

Food truck with built-in kitchen. A friend of mine has a food truck the size of a UPS truck that was converted into a kitchen on wheels. It has a 6,500-watt generator on the back of it that powers everything. The inside consists of two big fryers, a large gas oven, refrigerator, double sinks, long stainless steel counter top, microwave oven, and a ventilation exhaust fan system to do away with the smoke. He and his family go into underprivileged communities and feed over two hundred fried fish and chicken meals at no charge and share the love of Christ with them. He also uses his truck for big secular events in the city, charging five to six dollars a plate to make an honest living as well.

Rent a large projector and show a movie. We tried this in an apartment complex many years ago. The movie was *The Cross and the Switchblade,* the real-life story of David Wilkerson and Nicky Cruz. To our amazement, about 150 people showed up to watch this movie, and the altar call afterward drew about 120 people to the Lord that night. When going this route, make sure you have very powerful speakers to project the sound properly.

Neighborhood outdoor carnival. Nothing draws young crowds like a carnival with games, large toys, vendors, prizes, fun activities, magic shows, music, food, and even fireworks. This type of event is sponsored yearly by our church during our annual picnic, which occurs in the parking lot of the church, and all the public is invited. It always culminates with fireworks. This is an excellent attention getter that you could use to your advantage to draw souls into the kingdom of our Lord.

Motorcycle ride for enthusiasts. This could be an excellent tool to gather motorcyclists together for a cause. You could gather as many motorcyclists as possible to travel a one- to three-hour trip—or longer. At the destination, have a sound system set up so you can minister to them about the love of Jesus, and follow it up with an altar call. The way you get the unsaved to participate is by an invitation of the believers to the unsaved motorcyclists. In the unsaved motorcyclist's mind, it's just a fun ride or trip, but in actuality, it is a setup for them to be introduced to Christ as Lord and Savior at the place of destination.

Have neighborhood blood drives. Not only would individuals come out to participate in saving the lives of needy people who might need blood, but also, as they are out to give blood, your church could pass out brochures or trinkets inviting them to attend your particular church service in a way that would not be soliciting.

Chapter 11

40 Excuses for Not Sharing Your Faith

1. **Intrusion of privacy.** Solution: Ezekiel 3:18, *"When I say unto the wicked, Thou shalt surely die; and thou givest him not warning, nor speakest to warn the wicked from his wicked way, to save his life; the same wicked man shall die in his iniquity; but his blood will I require at thine hand."* Individuals are sent to us by divine appointment, and we are to lead them to the Lord, but we often feel as though we might be intruding or trespassing on their beliefs. Real love for that individual will take the risk of being ridiculed and rejected to share Christ's love with them. What if you knew the bridge ahead were out and there was a 100-foot drop-off? Would you warn the individual, or feel you've intruded on his privacy and not say a word? Love risks rejection—love anyway—not to mention that God commands us to "Go ye...!

2. **Lack of biblical knowledge.** Prepare yourself, study, and mobilize yourself for use by the Lord. If you have trouble memorizing things, then simply write your Scriptures or your dialogue down on index cards and read them if necessary. Never let being ill-prepared stop you.

3. **Intimidation because of a bad name given to Christians.**
We can learn a lesson or two from Gandhi, who is reported to have said, "If the world had been introduced to the Christ of Christians, the world would have received him, but instead they have been introduced to the Christians of Christ, therefore they reject Him." Let people know that sure, many Christians have dropped the ball and messed up miserably. However, Jesus will never ever let them down if their eyes are fixed on Him.

4. **Ashamed or Embarrassed.** *Simple solution: Jesus said, "If you be ashamed of me before men, then I'll be ashamed of you before my Father in heaven"* (Mark 8:38). Notice how the Devil and his crowd are not ashamed of anything, but instead they parade their sin proudly and boastfully among the world. How dare we as the people of God allow such immorality to be openly celebrated before us with ridicule against us without sharing one word to win the lost?

5. **I don't feel this is the ministry God called me to walk in.**
It is not based on a feeling, but on obedience, according to Matthew 28:19–20. We don't feel like doing right all the time, but we must obey anyhow. God called all Christians into this **ministry of reconciliation** (2 Corinthians 5:18). This simply means that as Christians, we have the privileged duty to bring all unsaved individuals back into right standing with our heavenly Father by going after the harvest.

6. **I don't have the boldness.** Proverbs 28:1 tells us *"the righteous are bold as a lion."* Boldness is a virtue that gets stronger the more we practice it; in other words, we get more bold as we go, not when we sit and do nothing. We start off timid, but end up bold as a lion. Timidity is a normal feeling all believers experience, but don't settle there. In 2 Timothy

1:7, Paul declares that *"God hath not given us a spirit of fear, but of power, and of love, and of a sound mind."*

7. **This is not my personality.** Again, we must obey the command of God. Boldness develops in our personality as we become obedient to God's word.

8. **I don't at all feel led.** God has given us the ministry of reconciliation. It's not based on being led, but based on doing what we know to do through obedience. This spirit of apathy is also used as a tool of the Devil. Our flesh nature despises the things of God, but our spirit man on the inside hates anything contrary to the will of God. As stated in an earlier chapter, get the lead out of your britches and get out there regardless and do what God called the body of Christ to do. The more we walk in the Spirit, the more we subdue the nature of our flesh and please the Lord by doing His will.

9. **I can't relate in language; I don't talk Ebonics or the same hip-hop-type language as some young folks.** People are not concerned whether or not you're able to relate to them language wise, they just want to feel real love acted out. When we "Go ye..." as the Lord commanded us to go in His name, then it will be the anointing that breaks the yoke through our genuine love and compassion for people, not the talk we talk.

10. **I can't relate in culture; I'm white and live among blacks.** In Galatians 3:28, the Bible tells us that *"there is neither Jew nor Greek...bond nor free...male nor female: for ye are all one in Christ Jesus."* One's skin color does not matter when it comes to the kingdom of God, because we are all one in the Lord. Unfortunately, sometimes down here on earth the color of skin does matter to people who walk in

ignorance or prejudice taught to them as little children growing up. However, I'm more convinced now than ever that God's *agape* love conquers all hard hearts. Whatever race or culture you belong to down here on earth, God's unconditional love practiced from a broken and contrite heart will always prevail over sin and hatred. Try it: you'll be totally surprised.

11. **I'm black and live among whites.** Same as above.

12. **I'm Anglo and live among Spanish-speaking people.** Same as above also. The only difference is the language barrier if you don't speak Spanish. Through new technology, there are apps on smartphones and tablets that will allow you to speak into it in English, and another language of your choosing will be translated. Let's take advantage of technology and win people to Christ no matter what.

13. **My testimony is boring and dull; I did not commit too many bad sins in life; I was a good sinner.** Then your testimony is that God kept you from bad sins. Wow, how many people do you know who can say the same? Your testimony is what you and you alone have experienced in life. You'll be surprised how many people like yourself can relate to your "boring, good sinner" lifestyle. Don't be ashamed, simply tell people the truth about how the Lord Himself has delivered you from your ugly situation, regardless of how bad or good it may have been for you.

14. **My testimony is too messed up and graphic; I did it all.** Your past is just that, your past. No matter how graphic or immoral your testimony might be, people can always relate to what you have experienced. The Bible says in 1 Corinthians 6:9–11 (ASV) *"Or know ye not that the unrighteous shall not inherit the kingdom of God? Be not deceived:*

neither fornicators, nor idolaters, nor adulterers, nor effeminate, nor abusers of themselves with men, nor thieves, nor covetous, nor drunkards, nor revilers, nor extortioners, shall inherit the kingdom of God. And such were some of you: but ye were washed, but ye were sanctified, but ye were justified in the name of the Lord Jesus Christ, and in the Spirit of our God." A good "Hallelujah!" would be appropriate now.

15. **I'm too busy; my job and my schedule won't allow me the time right now.** No wonder your life is topsy-turvy now, for you are too busy for God. You must make time to obey him by putting first things first in your life. You may think things are going great for you now, but give it a little time. If you know to do better, then do it. If not, you're playing with fire when you try to talk your way out of the will of God. The Bible says it this way in Hebrews 10:31 (ASV) *"It is a fearful thing to fall into the hands of the living God."*

16. **I can't talk about God or Jesus where I work, I'll be fired.** Then talk about Him during lunch break or before work starts, or even after work hours. Ask the one you are trying to witness to for a phone number to call him later. But by all means, respect your job's protocol and don't put yourself in a situation of being fired because you ministered to or witnessed to people during the time you were on your job's time clock. This is a bad witness for a Christian. Respect their rules, and do this for the Lord on your free time. This way Satan can't bring any legitimate charges against you, only false ones, in which case the Lord Himself will be your defense.

17. **I have too many demons in my own life to fight.** Well, welcome to Life 101. *"For all have sinned, and come short of the glory of God"* (Romans 3:23). Absolutely none of us are perfect or have all things 100 percent together in our lives.

Maybe if we admit this to more unsaved people, they might respect us even more, because many Christians appear to be absolutely perfect to other individuals. All Christians fall short, but this does not at all give us as believers a license to go out and practice sin, either. If we believers practice sin, we are indeed no different from the unsaved sinner. They are called sinners because they do just that, they practice sin. Remember to practice being faithful and ask God to forgive you every time you do sin, and forsake that sin in your own life. When we approach others, we must come in humility, not pride and judgment, because this causes the unsaved person to put up red flags in his mind when he sees us approaching. As you hear yourself talk about God's word to people, it will convict you even more to live rightly, because His word is a two-edged sword that cuts both ways. It cuts the people we are talking to by convicting them, and it cuts us as it leaves our mouths. Doing the "Go ye…" command keeps us on the straight and narrow and causes us to continue to take inventory of our own lives consistently.

18. **I'm old and can't relate to young folks.** In 1 John 2:13 the Bible says, *"I write unto you, fathers, because ye have known him that is from the beginning."* Your wisdom can help a generation in more ways than you can even imagine. By the way, this applies to older women in the Lord as well. Why is it that you are still holding on all of this time? I know without a doubt that you are to pass the baton of wisdom down to the next generation so that people in this godless society in which we live can see firsthand from your personal experiences how God can and will bless our lives and deliver us from whatever circumstances hold us in captivity. **You are that living legend, sir or ma'am!**

19. **I'm young and can't relate to older folks.** In 1 John 2:14 the Bible says, *"I have written unto you young men, because*

ye are strong, and the word of God abideth in you, and ye have overcome the wicked one." You as a young person, male or female, can help older folks to know Christ in their old age. You walk in and abide in a strength that older people depend upon. They can relate to life in more ways than you'll ever know. Sin today mirrors sin in their earlier years; it's just more prevalent because of things such as the Internet and other divisive tactics that the Devil concocted. Many older people have often been totally forsaken, neglected, forgotten, or ignored by their so-called loved ones. They would love more than anything just to sit down and share with someone who will take the time to listen to them. Not all older people are Christians, as you well know, so this is a wonderful time to take advantage of the opportunity as it presents itself to share Christ with that individual while time stands still for them.

20. **I'm not intellectual like those around me.** Just be yourself and share the love of Christ. It is the Holy Spirit and God's Word that will convict the person with whom you're trying to share. Some intellectuals are so prideful they shut down and will not receive from certain people of "lower" levels of intellect. Imagine how Paul the apostle must have felt before King Agrippa or Festus in Acts 26. Paul walked with such an anointing upon him that King Agrippa confessed to Paul he was almost persuaded to become a Christian. The anointing of God upon your life can take you to higher places your intellect can't even reach. Praise be to God!

21. **I'm too intellectual to relate to hoodlums.** This is indeed an attitude of pride. There are seven things God despises and considers as abominations in Proverbs 6:16–19, and a proud look is number one on that list. God completely hates pride, and for a Christian to think he or she is above witnessing to anyone is just a slap in God's face. Humility

says, "because I am a Christian and God has blessed me with wisdom from on high, I'll share with those less fortunate the wisdom that God has given me and win their soul to Christ." *"For he that winneth souls is wise"* (Proverbs 11:30). Street people who lived a hard life know real love when they see it and in the long run appreciate it.

22. **I hang around Jews who don't believe in Jesus as Savior.** Show them proof of Jesus throughout the Old Testament in types and shadows. Of course, this takes a well-learned student of the Word of God to be able to persuade them, but if they won't accept, then let your life be a living example of Christ's love, integrity, and character. Continue to intercede consistently in prayer for them that their eyes might be opened to the truth that Jesus is God in the flesh and that He is the only way to get to heaven.

23. **I'm around the worst sinners who will not listen to me because they despise Christians.** The effective way to deal with this type of scenario is to apologize to them on behalf of all Christians who have been judgmental or condescending to them. Don't condemn them no matter how vulgar their lifestyle may be. Since they are not willing to listen to you as you try to reach them for Christ, you must let your light shine bright to them every day so they will eventually see your good works and glorify God in heaven (Matthew 5:16). When calamity comes their way, you are probably the first person they will run to for help. When this happens, lovingly receive them with open arms, without the "I told you so" syndrome, and point them in the direction of the Lord.

24. **I'm around nothing but gays and lesbians who hate Christians.** The above advice applies to this scenario as well. A group of forty-plus Christian friends of mine went

131

with me to witness to gays and lesbians in Los Angeles on Sunset Boulevard. We went into over twelve night clubs that contained only gays and lesbians, and because of the love of Jesus that we exemplified, over seventeen souls were saved that same night, confessing Jesus Christ as their Savior and Lord. The key is showing them love, not condemnation. If they don't receive the Lord after that, patiently wait and continue to intercede on their behalf. Never give up praying for them no matter what. Remember, Jesus also told us *"not everyone will receive us, if not, then shake the dust off of your feet"* (Matthew 10:14) and go to the next one.

25. **I'm around folks who are into cults such as Islam, Buddhism, Jehovah's Witnesses, or Mormonism.** This might come as a shock to many people, and may even be a controversial thing to say, but the religions just mentioned are indeed cults and are diametrically opposed to the doctrine of Christianity in the details. Outwardly, things appear similar, and these religions even mention Christ in their teachings and respect Him as a holy man. However, the line is drawn when you ask if Jesus and God are one and the same, and if Jesus is indeed the only way to God the Father. Jehovah's Witnesses and Mormons might be viewed as a form of Christianity in a sense, but are also very deceptive and are not at all on one accord with the Christian Bible or our doctrine of beliefs. All of these cults have their different bibles. **Question:** How then do you win them to Christ, especially if they feel that what they believe is truth? The way you don't win them is by argument or trying to force them to believe your way. Never try to argue or defend the gospel, just live it and preach it if people will receive it. Read Romans 16:17–18 and Matthew 7:6. To inspire mankind to believe in our beloved Savior is to live your life above reproach among them and consistently walk in the love of God by way of your character. This will

make a mark on their lives, and they may even notice that most people in their cults don't quite handle life the way you do. This powerful witness, along with the Holy Spirit revealing to them the truth of God's Word, will help to win them over a period of time.

26. **I've made a mistake and I've fallen into sin as a Christian.** Am I now exempt from being qualified to share anything with anyone at all? No, you must first deal with your own sin through repentance and then forsake that particular sin. Read David's prayer in Psalm 51. After you've repented and forsaken that particular sin, then you can get others saved and even share your personal deliverance process with them. Expressing the Lord's forgiveness in your life when you fall short can sometimes bring them to Christ in a faster way than normal. They will see firsthand and understand that Christians are not superhuman, but are normal people trying to die to themselves everyday.

27. **I'm broke, busted, and frustrated myself, how can I tell someone else about Him?** Hang in there, and call things that are not as though they were into existence in your life, and in time God will bless your life abundantly. Remember Matthew 6:33 which says *"Seek ye first the kingdom of God, and His righteousness; and all these things shall be added unto you."* Your testimony is one in which a large number of the world's population can relate to, as they are also struggling with their finances. This also shows that you're not serving the Lord for only the loaves and the fishes—that is, for money or wealth. If you were, then you would have forsaken him by now because of your own personal situation. Let them know that even though you may not be where you want in the area of your finances, that God has given you a peace beyond your understanding, and a faith to know that He'll work all things out for your good.

28. **I'm sick and dying, I can't share with someone else because problems are too big for me.** If you have the right attitude, not only could Jesus heal you, but also bring people to Him faster because you believe Him regardless of your condition. You don't know the many times I have stood by the bedside of dying Christians with incurable sicknesses and diseases. While I came prepared to lift them up and to encourage them, several of them encouraged me instead. I even thought, *Lord, how is it that they can encourage me when they are in such a debilitated condition?* It is absolutely amazing to see how God Almighty can give peace to the dying to the degree that they encourage those of us who are still well to live on. I realize that not all sicknesses are unto death, however many are unto death, and those who suffer have an amazing kind of faith that the Lord gives them. These types of circumstances make it possible for the Lord to win unsaved friends and family members to Him through that broken vessel of God and their relentless faith and positive attitude. Remember what Paul the apostle said in Philippians 1:21,*"For me to live is Christ, and to die is gain."*

29. **People will think I'm too religious and start treating me like a perfect saint when I know that I am not perfect.** You must let them know according to Romans 3:23, *"all have sinned and come short of his glory."* Share with them that if it were not for the grace of Almighty God, you would be in a terrible sinful mess yourself and that you're not at all perfect, but are striving to be in every way. This testimony helps them understand that Christians are not Superman, but ordinary people in whom God has chosen to place His amazing Spirit. We serve a perfect God, who has a perfect Spirit, but chooses to use and work through imperfect vessels.

30. **People will wait for me to fall, so I don't witness because I don't want to let Jesus down if I do make a mistake.** Again, welcome to Life 101. As stated earlier, Romans 3:23 says *"All have sinned, and come short of the glory of God."* We as believers must convince the unsaved that there are no perfect people. You may look throughout the entire Bible and the only perfect one you'll find in there is the Lord Jesus Himself. So even if you did slip up and sin in an area, it is not at all the end of the world for you. That sin wasn't your first one, and it certainly won't be your last one, either. Stand up and be a witness for Jesus no matter what. This type of doubt is usually sparked by the enemy Satan himself to cripple us from opening our mouths to share Christ with others. **News Flash!** Even if you have never sinned a day in your life, the people of the world will still dislike you as a believer and will always have something negative to say about you, no matter what. They did it to Jesus who is perfect, what makes you think they won't dislike or even hate you and me? Remember, we have an obligation to the Lord, and that is to "Go ye...!" Let's just obey the Lord and trust that He'll indeed take care of the rest.

31. **I just don't know how to witness; I don't know what to say.** Just keep reading, and in the next few chapters, you'll discover valuable pointers to help you become an effective witness for Jesus. You will receive step-by-step instructions about what to say when faced with different scenarios for favorable results.

32. **I just got saved; I'm too new at this.** Tell them of your recent experience in getting saved. Let them know step-by-step how you came to know Jesus. Your testimony is a powerful tool, especially since you are new and fresh in your walk with Christ. This point is further discussed in Chapter 6, "My Personal Testimony."

33. **I just don't want to rock the boat; I want to be politically correct.** This is the same attitude the Pharisees had. You must step out of your comfort zone to allow the Holy Spirit to use you, and this means that sometimes you will indeed rock the boat. Not only will you rock the boat, but also you will be politically incorrect, without a doubt. But the question you need to ask yourself is this: "Is rocking the boat worth a soul or two being born again even if I'm hated and disrespected by many afterward?" Remember the words of missionary and poet C.T. Studd: "Only one life, 'twill soon be past. Only what's done for Christ will last."

34. **I'm a man, it doesn't seem appropriate for me to witness to a woman. Or, I'm a woman, it doesn't seem appropriate for me to witness to a man.** Says who, and why not? Galatians 3:28 states *"there's neither male nor female, for we are one in Christ Jesus."* Legalistic churches will teach and preach this type of nonsense, but this is not at all of God. When Jesus gave us the command to "Go ye…" He did not specify that women were not to talk to men and vice versa. In fact, you see Jesus himself ministering to women one-on-one several times in the Bible. There was Mary Magdalene and the woman at the well, just to name two. However, if you are bound and tied up in your life with the spirit of lust, you may need to talk one-on-one with your same gender until you feel in your heart that you are free from that weakness. There are times when you must apply wisdom in situations, especially when it comes to one-on-one witnessing to individuals of the opposite sex, particularly at night and alone in places not related to church. Situations like this could lead to temptations or could even be a setup from the enemy for a fall. That is why we must be sober and vigilant and watch out for our adversary the Devil (1 Peter 5:8).

35. **If I share my faith, I'll probably lose quite a few of my friends.** This is probably true for the most part; however, ask yourself, "What type of friend would I really be if my friends were to die and leave this planet without my sharing Jesus with them even one time?" Real friends love you no matter what. They love you even at the expense of losing your friendship if it will save your life. Sure, not all of your old friends will understand you, nor will all of them be willing to accept Christ into their lives right away. But you can't let them stop you from serving the Lord, or from loving them enough to share Christ with them. You may in fact have to go your own separate way, especially if you no longer have anything in common with them. Satan will use old friends to keep you from growing in the Lord, and to cause spiritual stagnation in your life. That is why for every friend you lose, God will bless you with new, godly friendships that will indeed be more meaningful and more productive for your life. You'll gain new Christians as lifetime friends. Keep in mind that birds of a feather will not only flock together, but also fly to the same destination. You are only as sharp as the friends you allow in your inner circle.

36. **I am seeking Christ but find it difficult to find Him for myself; how can I witness to others?** You really can't at this point. You must first and foremost be a born-again Christian yourself by the acceptance of Christ Jesus into your life. Then you must submit yourself under the leadership of a local Bible-based church and pastor so you can be taught and discipled as a strong and effective believer. As you develop a genuine love and passion for Christ, then at that point you will become qualified to share your personal testimony with others and rejoice with them as they too receive the Lord as Savior into their lives.

37. People I know believe there are too many hypocrites in the church to listen to me. That is why they need to take their eyes off hypocrites and look to Jesus instead. Remind them that man is fallible and will in fact let them down at times, but not Jesus. He will never, ever disappoint them in any way. When people with whom you try to share Christ tell you of the many hypocrites there are in church, just remind them that there may be a few in church here and there, but in hell, they are all there!

38. Several people believe the Bible contradicts itself; how do I deal with that? This is always a tactic the Devil will use to lead you on a wild-goose chase to evade the issue of the need for Jesus being in our lives as Lord and Savior. The Bible never contradicts itself; people just need a revelation of the Word of God to understand it correctly. Without being argumentative or too theological with them, just share with them the genuine love of God for them, and the need of repentance and the consequences of sin if one does not repent. If they still insist that you try to explain to them that there are contradictions in the Bible, then they are not at all ready to repent or receive Christ into their hearts, so don't waste your time, and by all means, don't get into a debate with them no matter what happens. In this case, you must shake the dust off of your shoes and move on to the next person.

39. Since God knows everything that there is to know, and he has already predestined us and knows who goes to heaven or to hell, why waste the time to try to minister to people who are stubborn and don't want to even hear the truth? Well, people must still have a chance to receive or reject Christ. The Bible asks the question, *"How then shall they call on Him in whom they have not believed? And how shall they believe in Him of whom they have not heard? And how shall they hear without a preacher?"* (Romans 10:14). You and

I are the preachers sent for them to have the opportunity to either receive or reject Him. God won't rain down any destruction or judgment on a people or a person until He first warns them. Though he already knows the outcome, He still gives every individual an equal chance to accept Him because He's *"not wishing that any should perish, but that all should come to repentance"* (2 Peter 3:9, ASV).

40. **Out of all the religions in the world with now over seven billion people on the planet, who is to say what I as a Christian believe is true, over all the other religious beliefs out there?** Notice that all of the other religions of the world teach lessons for you to take in through knowledge of your mind or psyche. They all have their rules and regulations to follow based upon the experience of the god(s) to whom they serve or pay tribute. Many of these cults or religions practice doing works and even have stipulations such as prejudices against other nations, people, or cultures. However, Christianity is not even a religion, but a relationship with the Savior of the world, Jesus Christ. He does not try to deal with knowledge of the mind, but rather deals with the wickedness of the heart and transforms a stony heart into a heart of flesh full of love and forgiveness of others. Christianity is God's love toward the entire world at large. This is the only religion—we'll just call it that for the sake of argument—that has the Holy Spirit working in the hearts of man convicting mankind of sin so he would be set free from sin and have eternal life. **Christ is the focus of our belief.** John 3:16 says it best; *"For God so loved the world that He gave His only begotten Son, that whoever believes in Him shall not perish, but have everlasting life"* (NKJV). Of all of the religious beliefs in the world, no other offers the totality of love, life, forgiveness, and acceptance of all peoples, kindreds, and cultures like that of Christianity. After all, nobody else out there died for all the world except Christ.

Brace yourself for the last three chapters ahead, and make up no more excuses from now on! You are about to graduate from average to superior in your soul-winning tactics. So get ready to receive your marching orders along with the proper tools and spiritual equipment to get the job done!

Chapter 12

Preparations for Your Soul-Winning Strategy: Get on Your Mark!

Inevitably, when most church leaders train a new covert along with those more experienced in Christ on how to witness to souls, how to share their faith, how to become an effective soul winner, how to save the lost, how to make fishers of men or disciples of men, whatever terminology you may be accustomed to using or hearing, they almost always give the individual some type of ABCs of soul winning format to follow step-by-step. After all, if one is embarrassed, afraid of rejection, feeling awkward or even unsure of himself—these are all normal feelings, especially if you are totally new at this—a makeshift, homemade type of approach could actually help to defuse these uncertainties somewhat. The only problem with this method is that while it could help those who are not used to doing this sort of thing, it could also possibly cripple a person and leave him walking in a mechanical state of mind as he tries to lead people to the Lord out of duty and flesh instead of love, passion, and experience from the heart. Let me explain myself further.

A little later in the next chapter, I will share with you common methods of soul winning, but the purpose for sharing this information is not for you to copy these methods verbatim, but to personalize these methods and use them from your heart as you see fit. Let these methods become a part of you, not your becoming a part of a method.

Ask yourself the ultimate question, "How would Jesus do it?" Would He approach people He never knew and say to them, "I'm here to tell you about me, because you are on your way to a living hell because of your sin, you dirty rotten sinner!" Of course not. Jesus actually showed us how to do exactly what he commanded us to do, "Go ye...!" Jesus had a unique way of befriending people and talking with them on their level. For instance, he would approach Peter and Andrew who were fishermen, and talk fish talk to them and compare their catching fish to their catching the souls of men. He would talk with those who were farmers and agriculturalists about a sower who went to sow seeds and how some fell by the wayside and so forth. He would talk to a woman guilty of adultery drawing water from a well about the living water he could offer her; that when she drinks of this water, she will never thirst again. He would do this without ever condemning her of her sin. He would talk at night with a Pharisee by the name of Nicodemus—the original Nick at Night—who approached him and let him know that *"Except a man be born again, he cannot see the kingdom of God."* And then go on to show further and tell him how this process takes place. *"Except a man be born of water and of the Spirit, he cannot enter into the kingdom of God. That which is born of the flesh is flesh; and that which is born of the Spirit is spirit"* (John 3:3–7).

The point I am trying to make is that Jesus had a way of reaching each person or group of people uniquely and differently depending on their circumstances, background, occupation, their calling or vocation in life. We can't be rigid and just hold to a certain plan for everyone we meet. If so, we'll only be able to reach a certain type of a person, limiting ourselves tremendously. Abraham H. Maslow wrote, "It is tempting, if the only tool you have is a hammer, to treat everything as if it were a nail." Guess what: not all of life's problems are like nails at all.

The big question is, **how do I personally win a soul unto the Lord if this is my very first time trying to succeed at this?** How do I start the conversation and what do I say? Before I get into the meat of explaining this to you, let me disarm any fears or trepidations that may exist. **Relax, and simply be yourself.** Trust me, I can't emphasize this enough, be yourself! People who never met you before can tell whether or not you are sincere. If you are used to seeing other Christians approach individuals with ease and calmness, it is because they are at ease and calm; you should be also. Your goal is to share Jesus Christ, the light of the world, with other people you may not know, but in a relaxed way by first befriending that person and again simply by being yourself. Not everybody you meet will be willing to listen to what you have to share with them. In fact, some may easily be offended and extremely rude to you. Expect victory, but prepare for rejection in case it happens.

Pray, Pray, Pray!

Billy Graham was once asked, "What is the secret to revival?" To everyone's amazement, he responded in three short answers:

1. Pray!
2. Pray!
3. Pray!

We as Christians oftentimes underestimate the very power of prayer altogether. As Jesus commanded us to "Go ye…" in Matthew 28:19–20, He wanted us to first be equipped.

One main way to be equipped is to be prayed up! We must bombard heaven through prayer before going out to any person to witness to him or share our faith with him. By this I mean that we must know this assignment is of God and not just something that has been concocted in our minds. Remember, Satan our archenemy is not willing to just turn people loose; he's actually trying to take them out by blinding them to the truth of God's word and keeping them in darkness so hell will be their fate. This is why there must be heavenly intervention and spiritual warfare first through our prayers.

The Bible tells us in 2 Corinthians 4:3–4: *"But if our gospel be hid, it is hid to them that are lost: In whom the god of this world hath blinded the minds of them which believe not, lest the light of the glorious gospel of Christ, who is the image of God, should shine unto them."*

Satan will in fact invade entire regions or areas with spiritual darkness where there is an infestation of crime, degradation, proliferation of sins, not to mention apostasy. We must do spiritual warfare by praying for that person, neighborhood, or region before even approaching. Our prayer must be for God to open the eyes of them who are blind that they may see and receive the love of Jesus in their hearts, and that the Lord would meet all of the needs in that individual's life, spiritual, financial, and physical. Remember what the word of the Lord says concerning warfare, in Ephesians 6:10-12: *"Finally, my brethren, be strong in the Lord, and in the power of his might. Put on the whole armor of God, that ye may be able to stand against the wiles of the devil. For we wrestle not against flesh and blood, but against principalities, against powers, against the rulers of the darkness of this world, against spiritual wickedness in high places."*

This should be a clear sign and wake-up call for all to know that soul winning or fulfilling the Great Commission by going forth through obedience requires much preparation through prayer. Our fight is not at all with people, but with the one behind people bringing about havoc and destruction, the Devil.

Read what the Lord tells us in Matthew 16:19: *"And I will give unto thee the keys of the kingdom of heaven: and whatsoever thou shalt bind on earth shall be bound in heaven: and whatsoever thou shalt loose on earth shall be loosed in heaven."*

This simply means that as believers in the Lord Jesus Christ, we've been given authority to bind and loose things on this earth. If we bind the enemy Satan from his tactics and his deceptive ways, then he'll be bound in heaven also. If we don't bind him, neither will God bind him; that authority has been allocated to us as believers.

Fasting is also a powerful tool to see exponential results. This should of course be done along with prayer to get biblical results. See Isaiah 58, known as the fasting chapter. The Bible in Daniel 11:32 says *"but the people that do know their God shall be strong, and do exploits."*

Dos and Don'ts to Be Aware of in Winning Souls

Before we actually take the plunge into fulfilling the Great Commission of "Go ye..." there are some practical dos and don'ts that must be dealt with for a total order of excellence and success.

First and foremost, keep in mind that salvation is in the acceptance of Jesus Christ into the heart of an individual, not particularly joining your church. **Salvation is in the person Jesus Christ, not a church, belief or doctrine.** By this, I mean that it is indeed important for the new believer to attend church, but your purpose in going forth is not primarily to introduce the individual to your church or pastor, but to introduce him to Christ. Satan would like more than anything for us to be unfocused, or to take the focus off the Savior Christ and to focus on a church or doctrine instead.

From personal experience over the years, I've noticed that

various new Christian converts are sometimes so enamored by the choir, musicians, and good preaching that they have somewhat of a subservient mentality toward the pastor and many leaders. Showing admiration and respect toward a pastor can be normal and even honorable, but the focus of everything in the atmosphere and setting of any church should be to honor, worship, and revere the Lord Jesus Christ. If pastors don't steer new young converts in this direction, they can set themselves up to be Jesus to that new believer. As a result, the new convert might look to them for everything rather than building up a healthy and holy relationship with our beloved Savior. Regardless of how wonderful and awesome your church might be, the focus and main reason for going out into the highways and hedges to compel people to come is for them to come to Jesus just as they are. The Lord Himself will pick them up from where they are and prepare to bring them up to the level that He has planned for them.

Second, avoid all arguments and debates that people will try to throw your way. Stay on track and realize that arguments are simply tactics the Devil uses to try to break our focus and our message of salvation to a lost and dying world. In Scripture, Jesus never tells us to defend the gospel in any way, but that the gospel is *"the power of God unto salvation to everyone that believeth"* (Romans 1:16). The Bible says in Matthew 7:6 (AB) *"Do not give that which is holy (the sacred thing) to the dogs, and do not throw your pearls before hogs, lest they trample upon them with their feet and turn and tear you in pieces."* Further corroboration of this Scripture is one found in Romans 16:17–18 (TLB) *"And now there is one more thing to say before I end this letter. Stay away from those who cause divisions and are upsetting people's faith, teaching things about Christ that are contrary to what you have been taught. Such teachers are not working for our Lord Jesus but only want gain for themselves. They are good speakers, and simpleminded people are often fooled by them."* Satan will always have someone planted in your path who is opposed to Christianity in some way or another to add confusion and difficulty. Don't be threatened by this ploy or be afraid, Instead, be encouraged because this proves that you are on the right track, otherwise Satan wouldn't waste his time through opposition. Keep in mind, if someone argues with you, it only proves that he is not yet ready to accept Jesus. Kindly walk away and go on with your assignment to the next prospect. If individuals become belligerent toward you or your group, completely ignore them and walk away. Luke 9:5 says, *"And whosoever will not receive you, when ye go out of that city, shake off the very dust from your feet for a testimony against them."*

Third, always make the individual you are ministering to feel as though he is really important to Jesus because in actuality, he is. This disarms one from all red flags that he may have held over us. Make him feel as if he is right and agree with him even if you know for a fact that he is dead wrong. The Bible even bears this out in Matthew 5:25. You want to correct an individual in love if he is in any major error, but only if he will receive it without any resistance, bitterness, or anger. Have a conversation with him, not a sermon. Quoting too many Scriptures to an unsaved person practicing sin in his life can be a serious turn-off. Understand that he in his present state is without Christ, and he cannot relate to too many Scriptures being hurled at him rapidly. You befriend him through conversation. Tell him of the love of Jesus by using instances in your own testimony.

Let him know to look to Jesus, and not bad hypocritical examples of Christians. I've used this before, but it bears repeating: Mahatma Gandhi is quoted as saying, "If the world had been introduced to the Christ of Christians, then the world would have received him, but instead they have been introduced to the Christians of Christ, therefore the world rejects him." What a sad commentary and misrepresentation of true believers, but it's true in some cases. Unfortunately, this is why it is difficult sometimes for Christian believers to succeed, due to hypocritical practices done by other believers. We tell people to live one way, but sometimes break all the rules as if the law of God doesn't apply to us. The world sees this hypocrisy and this becomes a major turn-off to many individuals, along with the condescending, self-righteous attitudes that some Christians may have. Remember, the Pharisees in the New Testament were the same way, and they were a major thorn in the side of Jesus.

Many times the individual you are witnessing to may use curse words or vulgarities. If this occurs, please don't take it personally or even be offended by these vulgarities. It comes with the territory. Remember, they don't know Jesus just yet and sinners will be sinners. They practice sinning and this is simply their nature. This was also our nature before Christ came in and redeemed us from our sins. By reacting in a way of shock, we make them feel uneasy and uncomfortable. Remember, we must catch the fish before we can clean it.

Fourth, your attitude should be one of joy and excitement, passion, raw enthusiasm and fire, one of challenge and adventure, one of ecstasy and rejoicing all mixed in together. If one expects to go out and lead a person or even a group of people to the Lord without excitement and passion, then one's purpose is already defeated. You are in no way ready to lead a person to the decision of the acceptance of Christ if you are uninterested, bored, fearful, or doing something because you feel this is to be done out of duty and obedience. If you are at this point, where you feel this is something to be done just out of sheer duty, then you may need to sit this one out, because you are not quite ready at this point in your life to fulfill the Great Commission. Even if you fall short and are not prepared due to lack of maturity and compassion, you are still responsible, and God holds you in contempt if you have not mobilized yourself.

In the book of Acts, the disciples were filled with passion and the love of Jesus, which in many cases got them in trouble through beatings, imprisonment, and even death. Think about it: What would cause individuals to continue to preach and share the good news of our beloved Savior, knowing that their lives could be snuffed out at any time. Trust me, this is the greatest high one can experience. Unlike that from an alcohol bottle, or a euphoric feeling from drugs that leaves you totally empty, this kind of high leaves you up as long as you want it to, and the more you do it, the more ecstasy you experience in the Lord. There is absolutely no other feeling comparable to winning a lost soul into the kingdom of God and snatching a soul out of the grips and the clutches of Satan from the eternity of hell and death to life eternal in Christ.

Think of it this way: What if your child, children, or even a loved one grew up not knowing the Lord? This means Satan would be their god, controlling their lives to the very fullest. How would you feel if you knew your kids or loved ones were marked by the Devil or on their way to an eternal hell? All you could do is pray and trust the Lord for their salvation and deliverance, not knowing how long it would take, or even if they would take heed if they were severely warned. Your children or loved ones would be in the same shape as the prodigal son. But when the prodigal son returned home after a long while, there was a lot of rejoicing and praise unto the Lord, because that son who had been a victim of sin and degradation had finally come to his senses and returned home to his father. What ecstasy and excitement!

How would you react if you and your spouse prayed for years for the salvation of that loved one who seemed to be getting worse instead of better? Then all of a sudden, one day their blind eyes were opened because someone took the time to share Jesus with them and led them in the prayer of salvation. Now all they want to do is to please the Lord in every way. What a feeling of jubilation!

This is indeed what life is all about. The reward of winning a soul or even seeing a loved one come home to his heavenly Father is even greater than you can ever imagine—and to think, the Lord used you to do it when he could have used anyone else on the planet. Look at it this way: of all of the jobs on planet Earth that people work at to get a paycheck, this is a job given to you and issued by our Father in heaven and tailor-made to fit your personality. God is your boss, and your pay and benefits are literally out of this world!

Last, try to be as approachable and transparent as possible and not too spiritual, which could inadvertently make an unsaved person feel dirty or even unworthy. This type of demeanor is a serious turn-off to the unsaved population. While you think you may be the holy one with their answer, you must keep in mind that our beloved Savior Jesus came on the level of every sinner with whom he had contact. He's our example. If Jesus Himself came down to the level of the common sinner, what makes you and me feel we are better than Christ? Sinners felt self-worth and received their identity after talking with Jesus and being in His presence. You and I are the only Jesus this world will ever see. They must see Christ in us, the hope of glory! **Now let's get you moving in the next chapter so you can finally receive your marching orders.**

CHAPTER 13

Get Mobilized for Attack: Get Set!

Now that you've read this far without throwing the book down proves that you have been arrested by the Holy Spirit and have an unquenchable desire to fulfill the Great Commission of "Go ye...!" Get ready for an experience in Christ that far surpasses anything else you might have deemed a euphoric feeling of ecstasy.

First and foremost, I'd like to introduce you to a technique of soul winning that proved to be effective throughout the first-century church in the book of Acts. This is the foundational way of fulfilling the "Go ye" plan of the Lord. This technique is simply known as the one-on-one soul-winning technique. It is pretty much self-explanatory, in that "each one is to reach one." One-on-one ministry is contagious and infectious. By this, I mean that every believer who has confessed Jesus Christ as Lord of his life should pass on his experience to the next person like a cold or a virus is passed on. If we have a direct relationship with the Father in heaven, then one-on-one ministry should be a direct result of being in His presence. First vertical relationship with God our Father through prayer and Bible reading, then horizontal relationships with our fellow man should be established whereby we introduce the world to our Father in heaven one-on-one. Remember vertical is up and down and horizontal is left and right. Vertical and horizontal together form a cross.

In fulfilling Jesus' command of "Go ye..." as discussed in the very first chapter of this book, **our primary goal is threefold: win them, teach and train them (discipleship), then send them out to make disciples of others**. If each believer in church would just win one person to the Lord using the one-on-one technique, and invite that one person to church to be taught of the Lord and discipled, then your church would double in size in a very short period of time. Let's say that each new convert were taught, discipled, and sent out to win another. Then a church would triple in size because multiplication would take place. Every single pastor would undoubtedly have to build a bigger church, and a worldwide revival would be inevitable.

Jesus did it, the disciples did it, and it spread like wildfire. Think about that for a minute: When fire spreads from one item to the next, it never diminishes, but only gets larger and stronger and will even get out of control if not contained. And so it is with us as Christians. If we each win a soul by the one-on-one technique, we'll never diminish, but we'll be even more on fire for the Lord as we follow His command of "Go ye...!" Others would also catch on fire because they will be infected by the heat and illumination of the Lord upon us and revival would be birthed. **We, like fire, will diminish only when we don't spread** but just sit contained in a box, the church, doing absolutely nothing. All of the following approaches will start off with the foundational method of one-on-one ministry. If we do things God's way according to the biblical pattern in the book of Acts, then we will get God's results without a doubt.

Charged up with AMPs

You were made aware of the dos and don'ts of the "Go ye..." command, so now let's get our plan of attack in order. **The entire purpose of this book is to prepare you for what is now about to be discussed.** To carry out our marching orders from the Holy Ghost, our commander in chief, we must follow a plan. In the book of Acts 2:3–4, the Bible says, *"And there appeared unto them cloven tongues like as of fire, and it sat upon each of them. And they were all filled with the Holy Ghost, and began to speak with other tongues, as the Spirit gave them utterance."* Here it is, the defining moment. Every time I read this Scripture in the Bible, I get chill bumps all over me, and I'm sure that group in the upper room must have experienced what felt like the electrical voltage of the Holy Spirit go up and down their bodies, inside and out. They were all so filled with the Holy Ghost that the fire bubbled up out of them in the form of tongues, that is, different languages. Electrical current is measured in amps, and no doubt they felt the Holy Ghost like a current. So to plan our soul-winning strategy, I'd like to use as an acronym the word **AMP—Approach, Message, Persuasion.** During the remainder of this chapter and in the final chapter, you'll be trained on how to master your Approach in different circumstances, what Message we are to share, and the Persuasion of leading one to the sinner's prayer. These are the AMPs of the Holy Ghost!

Approach

Approach is the act of drawing near or coming within range. It's the method used or steps taken in setting about a task.

In this section, we will discuss different ways of approaching individuals, groups of people, and even massive gatherings of souls for a harvest toward obedience to the Great Commission, "Go ye…!" Here is a nugget of truth: **Our attitude determines our approach, and our approach determines our success or failure.** With this in mind, we must remember that we are the hands, feet, and even the mouthpiece of our beloved Savior. Our demeanor, frame of mind, and overall way we respond should denote the very character and nature of Jesus. This could be summed up as our attitude. With that in mind, our approach will automatically disarm any questionable demeanors we might face. We will discuss seven approaches or methods: **Confrontational Approach, Befriend Approach, Sympathy Approach, X-Ray Approach, Survey Approach, Cyberspace Approach, and Massive Outreach Approach.** Each one of these is designed to ensure your success and victory in your "Go ye…" endeavor.

Confrontational Approach

We meet people by the wayside in life as we pass by them. Any of these individuals could be our next assignment in sharing the message of the gospel. This is also a one-on-one method of ministry. This approach is usually short-term. You'll know it's God leading you, because your spirit will feel a tug of the Holy Spirit telling you to share with him or her. Even if you are very new to this, the Holy Spirit knows how to get your attention. He knows exactly where you live. If it seems that you may have missed His voice the first time, trust me, there will indeed be plenty more opportunities. This is not based on the way a person may appear to look on the outside, nor is it based on the race or gender of the person, but based solely on a witness of the Holy Spirit leading you. At this point, you must confront him or her in casual conversation. "Then how, and what do I say?" I'm so glad you asked. Here are some examples:

"Hello sir (or ma'am), as I passed by you, I noticed that you stood out a bit because you look like a person of distinction who knows where you are going in life. Am I right so far?" If his answer is "I'm not sure," then you confront him by telling him his purpose and identity which lies in Christ. Remember to relax and let it flow from the purity of your heart. Keep in mind that you should already have prepared yourself and familiarized yourself with Scriptures to be able to share with him and relate to him in a way concerning his destiny and identity that doesn't sound too preachy. The Holy Spirit is in control at this point, so yield to Him. Let him know that he will never, ever know who he really is until he knows who HE is! If he tells you that he does in fact know where he is going in life, then ask him to explain. If he leaves Jesus out of the equation, then let him know that it will not work with self-effort alone, but by the grace of God though a yielded life.

Here's another example of this approach: "Hello sir, that surely is a sharp suit you have on," or "Hello miss, I sure do like that outfit. Would you mind if I asked you where you got it? Because you look like a million dollars." Allow them to respond. Then say something like, "Speaking of a million dollars, what if I told you that you've just won the lottery and it were real?" Allow them to share their answer to the question, and your response would be something like, "If you allowed Jesus to come into your heart, you've done a whole lot better than hit the jackpot or lottery. When He becomes Lord in your life, He'll give you riches, honor, long life, peace, and much, much more without any regret or sorrow attached." These are just a few examples of how you can lovingly confront an individual without sounding too preachy or religious. You can create your own scenarios or conversational techniques that will catapult you into deeper levels and realms of the Holy Spirit. These examples are just templates for you to follow to help you with your own creativity.

Befriend Approach

Unlike the Confrontational Approach, which is a short-term approach, this is **more of a long-term approach.** It's best used when we interact with people on a regular basis over a protracted period of time. We become very familiar with them. We are familiar with their good habits, their bad habits, their character flaws, sins in their lives that they might practice on a daily basis, and even vulgarities that might spew out of their mouths on several occasions. We can't have a superior attitude over people like this, because we ourselves were like this in many ways before the Lord Jesus redeemed us from the very curse of sin. Thanks be to God! The world will be the world: they curse, talk dirty talk, and are irascible. But we must befriend them and show them a better way. We must be wise to win them. These are usually people whom we've known over a long period of time from the neighborhood in which we live, people with whom we work on our jobs, friends we've met during our school years, and folks we've known from childhood. Because they are very familiar with us and our personal ways due to being around us for long periods of time, we are more apt to being received by these people than by anyone else since they know us better. Therefore all red flags will be disarmed and their hearts will be more open for the gospel of Christ to be preached to them.

By befriending them, we allow the love of Jesus to flow through our lives. We never have a condescending or judgmental attitude toward them because they're as real as it gets from our point of view. In short, we know several people in our lives who fit this category. It may be that in all the years we've known them, the Lord was setting them up for the biggest show of all, that is, the truth of the gospel being unveiled before them in a witness of our personal lives and testimonies.

Sympathy Approach

This is one of the most opportune approaches to use when it comes to the soul-winning strategy. Every human being at some point in life goes through some type of crisis that may affect him in a way that seems unbearable. These situations or crises may involve the loss of a job, a car breakdown, sickness, death, divorce, embarrassment, serving jail time, humiliation, foreclosure, or even abandonment. This type of approach from a distance might seem as if one were taking advantage of an individual while he was down on his luck, as it were, but in all fairness, these are opportunities to capitalize on through ministry in a good way. Let this sink in for a minute: People can indeed be down and out, but we are coming to them with good news to share with them at this crucial turning point of their lives. This allows the believer to approach the downtrodden with a listening ear.

Before calamity struck him, he may not have even given the time of day to a Christian, but God has him at a point of self-introspection in which He can intervene in his life through love and compassion. Moments like this can break the power of the Devil in half on one end, yet it could cause further damage and even suicidal thoughts on the other end. You've heard the saying "strike while the iron is hot." Well, this is the time to seize the moment in the life of a broken person. The truth of God's word could lift him up out of despair and bring him up to the level in God where he belongs, before Satan depresses him to a point of either not wanting to get help from any source or the threat of suicide.

God can use calamity to get our attention, and this could be the very open door for ministry that believers in Christ pray about to get the individual to come to a decision of acceptance of Jesus into his heart. This is not the time to tell a person in this predicament, "I told you so" or "I knew this would eventually happen to you." No, this is the time to share the very love and essence of our beloved Savior. Love indeed covers the multitude of sins. **Love needs to be expressed during the times individuals need it the least.** Let's see what God's word says about the subject of love.

> *Love is very patient and kind, never jealous or envious, never boastful or proud, never haughty or selfish or rude. Love does not demand its own way. It is not irritable or touchy. It does not hold grudges and will hardly even notice when others do it wrong. It is never glad about injustice, but rejoices whenever truth wins out. If you love someone, you will be loyal to him no matter what the cost. You will always believe in him, always expect the best of him, and always stand your ground in defending him. All the special gifts and powers from God will someday come to an end, but love goes on forever. (1 Corinthians 13:4–8, TLB)*

The Word of God teaches us that *"God is love"* (1 John 4:16). What a perfect platform we have before us to show individuals His love during this hour in their need. Jesus

Himself used the sympathy approach to win people. There was the woman at the well who was rejected by many, there was Zacchaeus who was hated by many because he was a tax collector, there was the harlot who washed Jesus' feet with her tears and dried them with her hair, and the list goes on and on. Jesus was cited as being *"a friend of publicans and sinners"* (Luke 7:34).

Jesus also gave the example of the good Samaritan, who poured oil and wine into the wounds of the man found by the roadside and left for dead (Luke 10:30–37). This man showed sympathy and compassion, taking care of that man as if he were a family member. He even had him put up in a hotel and the charges placed on his own tab. The Bible does not go into any further details than this, but do you think if the good Samaritan wanted to talk to the man about the acceptance of Jesus as his Lord and Savior that the man would have a problem listening to him? After the example of love and compassion the Samaritan showed him, I think not!

Let's be *"wise as serpents, yet harmless as doves"* (Matthew 10:16). When this opportunity presents itself, Christians should be on the very cutting edge, ready to help out a fellow man or woman when he or she is down so we can extend an arm of compassion to bring him or her from the bleeding side of Calvary to Christ, the hope of glory!

X-ray Approach

This one-on-one approach probes cunningly to find out where a person is located spiritually. Just as an X-ray machine acquires electromagnetic radiation images of the bone structure of the human body by use of wavelengths, our wavelengths are the signs, conversational terms, or gestures that individuals show us as we approach them through casual conversation.

Some negative responses are obvious and others not so obvious at all. Unlike the Confrontational Approach, in which we just engage in conversation, this approach probes into their responses to find out where they are located spiritually.

For instance, you may directly ask "Are you interested in spiritual things?" or "How do you feel about life after death?" or "Have you ever wondered if everyone who dies automatically goes to heaven or not?" or "Do you believe in heaven and hell?" These direct questions usually call for direct answers, and their responses let you know whether or not they are even remotely interested in the things of God.

Be a good listener. Be like a doctor who always asks questions to identify his patient's condition. If you detect any hint of resistance or hostility, then kindly end the conversation without allowing Satan to stir up an argument, and just gently walk away from that person, then move onto the next assignment or person. Remember, not every person with whom you come in contact is a ripe fruit ready to be harvested. However, if you discern interest or maybe a tender heart toward God, then move in on your message, and ultimately lead them to the Lord through the sinner's prayer. Persuading them to receive Christ into their hearts will be discussed in full detail in the next chapter.

Survey Approach

For whatever reason, when all else seems to falter, this approach can be used convincingly to get you out of any jam and into the amelioration of souls into the kingdom of God quite impressively. This approach is more effective if used in crowded settings such as malls, amusement parks or carnivals, outside university campuses, or even door-to-door in your community.

With this approach, you simply take a short survey by asking one person or even several people at a time six simple questions seemingly unrelated to anything dealing with Christianity. Then afterward your explanation to them will be extremely powerful and impacting as a witness unto the Lord.

The questions are as follows:

1. What is your number one goal in life?
2. Do you have a job?
3. Are you a homeowner?
4. Do you have any children?
5. Do you have life insurance?
6. Why do you feel you were born on this earth?

The explanations behind these six questions are as follows:

1. **I asked what your number one goal in life was because...** The purpose is to let them know that the Lord Jesus is a priority in life. *"But seek ye first the kingdom of God, and his righteousness; and all these things shall be added unto you."* (Matthew 6:33). If they have a plan in life that does not include the Lord at all, then ask, *"What does it profit a man, if he gains the whole world and loses his own soul, or what will a man give in exchange for his soul?"* (Matthew 16:26).

2. **I asked if you had a job because...** Explain that God the Father is our head boss and a very loving CEO in this life and the life to come in the kingdom of heaven. Convey to them that He has a very important task for them to cover for Him while they are here on this earth. Their job is to walk in their prophetic destiny, calling, or vocation that the Lord Himself has divinely set in motion for them down here on this planet by way of

the *Ministry of Reconciliation* (talked about on page 86). Furthermore, they are to teach others to also obey the Great Commission in their freedom of walking in the truth of God's Word through love.

3. **I asked if you were a homeowner because...** Tell them that accepting Jesus into their hearts guarantees them benefits out of this world—literally—such as their heavenly mansion. He has gone away to prepare a place for them and will be calling them home one day soon (John 14:2).

4. **I asked if you had any kids because...** I bet you would be willing to die for your kids to protect them if you had to, wouldn't you? Guess what? God died for His kids and protected us from hell and from death. Now He wants you to be His child down here on earth and represent Him well by confessing Him as Lord and Savior, so He can protect all of them that are His from the Devil's wrath and destruction.

5. **I asked if you had life insurance because...** Life insurance secures your family and loved ones only in this life in the event of your death. I'm more concerned whether or not you have eternal life insurance, which is guaranteed coverage and security in the hereafter. After all, statistics tell us one out of every one person will eventually die someday. The only way you get eternal life coverage is through the acceptance of Christ Jesus as your Lord and Master.

6. **I asked why you felt you were born on this earth because...** God has so much invested in you, and your true identity is in Him. But you won't really know who you are until you know who He really is. When you

discover who God really is through your relationship with Him by prayer, daily Bible reading and devotion, then your world will start to make sense because you'll discover who you really are by knowing Him.

This sums up the Survey Approach, but again, these examples are just a pattern to follow until the Lord begins to stir up the creative juices inside your own heart. Through much prayer, fasting, and planning, you just can't go wrong, but expect a mighty harvest of souls for the kingdom of God.

Cyberspace Approach

One of the most practical ways of winning the lost is via the Internet. Within the past twenty years, this world has moved rapidly toward an international communication system connecting the entire world together by way of the World Wide Web. With the widespread use of smartphones, iPads and other tablets, and similar mobile devices, our society is enthralled by communication networks such as Facebook, Twitter, and Youtube, just to name a few. People are also able to send text messages and e-mails to win the lost or even to encourage downtrodden individuals by way of the Internet.

Through this approach, we can personally minister to untold hundreds or even thousands of souls. We can use this approach further as a mechanism to invite people to different soul-stirring events that could change and revolutionize their lives, including Christian concerts, conferences, church services, plays, and even picnic-type events. Many people feel more comfortable with this approach, because often the person to whom you may be ministering may never physically see your face, although they could see your face if you choose to use something like Skype, FaceTime, or Google Hangouts. I could give countless testimonies of the many lives that were saved and ministered to through the use of the Internet by way of this Cyberspace Approach.

In the next and final chapter, we will discuss the last of the approach methods used, and probably the most powerful of all the approaches, the Massive Outreach Approach. Our Message and Persuasion discussed in the final chapter seals the entire deal. **Get ready for celebration because "the Devil's kingdom is coming down!"**

CHAPTER 14

Attack! Tear The Devil's Kingdom Down: "Go ye…!"

I n this final chapter, you will receive the proper tools to equip yourself fully in your "Go ye…" ventures dealing with Massive Outreach, the Message you are to deliver, and effective Persuasion for leading individuals to the confession of sins and praying the Prayer of Salvation unto the Lord Jesus.

Massive Outreach Approach

Not too many churches or individuals are fully mobilized and properly groomed for this final, yet efficacious and compelling approach. The Massive Outreach Approach has two different extremes: total triumph and victory that may even spark revival in a city or area, or embarrassing defeat due to lack of preparation and inadequacy. **Never under any circumstances have a novice lead a Massive Outreach program,** especially in a heavily populated area. Beginners should receive training on a smaller scale, led by a knowledgeable evangelist or pastor, to build up confidence and experience. In this way a beginner will learn how to respond to any given situation by taking charge, and how to bring things under control if they get out of hand, which indeed many times they do. This approach to soul winning targets the masses and could play a major part in inducting new converts into your local church.

As we tackle this approach, here are a few items worthy of discussion:

1. When planning your outreach, please don't spend time in dead areas or extreme conditions. Let me explain what I mean through this real-life example. Many years ago when I first joined my current church, the very first evangelist my pastor had leading the church in the area of outreach was a very loving woman of God, but she was extremely limited due to her lack of experience and training. This is not mentioned as an indictment or to attack her in any way, because her motives were indeed pure and her heart was right and tender before the Lord. She lacked experience, however, a point all of us face at some point in our lives. At that time, my pastor had a little more than 125 members, and that was his first year as pastor at this new facility. With this in mind, he could only use whoever at that time was available to evangelize.

We ventured out on our first major street service in downtown Atlanta. Much preparation had been made, and because of many announcements over the pulpit, the majority of the church was fired up and ready to go out and hit the streets. The only problem was that we endeavored to do this in the middle of the winter when the temperature was 22 degrees in Atlanta, one of the few times in history that Atlanta got that cold. To add insult to injury, the evangelist had scheduled us to minister in downtown Atlanta in an area deserted of people especially on an extremely cold evening. So we preached to ourselves that day and came back praising God about what a great time we had.

No souls were saved because there were no souls present to hear our message. Keep in mind, the whole purpose for going out on the streets to win souls is to fulfill the Great Commission of "Go ye," not to preach to each other. This is why location and weather conditions must be right. What type of success do you think one would have if he were to go out on the streets during inclement weather? What about sunshiny weather in the desert? An ideal case would be to minister in a neighborhood or location full of prospective souls during favorable weather conditions.

2. Know the demographics of the target area. Who are you speaking to? What type of group or people? What culture or race of individuals are you planning on speaking to? Is the neighborhood upscale or rundown? Does crime play a major factor in this particular location? Are there many homeless people nearby? These questions actually affect the way you prepare your outreach to that particular area. For instance, if the neighborhood or area you are planning to minister in is an upscale, highly respected neighborhood, you probably won't need to prepare meals to feed the hungry or pass out clothing for those less fortunate, but would need to prepare a message in your delivery of charity, morality, and the importance of returning to the Lord.

Also, the music you play might not be suitable to that particular community or gathering of people. They may in all honesty strongly dislike the type of Christian music that your group plans to play. After all, what is the primary goal, to minister and to reach ourselves or the lost souls in that particular community? Remember, we are trying to reach the unsaved world as a part of the Great Commission, not Christians who already know the Lord. So with that in mind, the music should cater to the demographics of the group you're trying to reach. One way to solve a problem if you're ministering to a multicultural group is to sing universal praise songs that minister to the general population of people at large. Put it this way, any music is better than nothing, but you would have more favorable results if you give them the style of Christian music they prefer to hear based on their culture.

On the other hand, if your chosen location is one of high crime and homelessness, then as bait, you need to have food baskets or hot meals to pass out, along with clothing. This way you will prove your sincerity and concern by meeting the needs of that community. After all, how can we hold someone's attention for any period of time spiritually, it we don't meet his or her current needs materially to the best of our ability?

3. Wait until after your program before you pass out anything! I've learned this rule over the years when it comes to passing out anything, whether it be food, clothing, or gifts. Human nature lets us know that people will be people and will come out only for the giveaways. After their immediate need is met, they will usually leave right away. You're not punishing the crowd by allowing them to sit through the entire program. After all, this is your bait used to get the masses out so you'll be able to minister to their physical as well as spiritual needs. If we did allow them to come out for the physical benefits alone, then we would not have an opportunity to minister to their spiritual needs or give an altar call, which allows them the opportunity to accept the Lord into their lives.

4. The best way to reach the masses is through a dependable working sound system with the proper number of speakers. A good and dependable public address system or lack thereof will make or break your success. Biblically speaking, Moses had a congregation to minister to which consisted of anywhere between one million and three million people. This is the question I always ask myself: "How did he communicate to the masses without a PA system during that time?" Well, the only way it could have been done is by the "pass the word along" system. This is when the people closest to him heard him, then they had to relay the message, sort of like a wave of communication through some sort of megaphone device to the ones behind them until it reached all of the crowds a mile or so away. Wow, can you imagine? By the time Moses was finished with his speech or sermon, he and Aaron were at home in their tents sleeping while his message still echoed because of such a large crowd.

Well, we have the Lord to thank dearly for modern-day technological advances such as PA systems and other kinds of loudspeakers by which we are able to amplify our voices to hundreds of thousands and even millions all at once. Now we are without excuse and need to utilize the electronic marvels that have been afforded to us, and go in the spirit of excellence to do exactly what the Lord called us to do.

It sometimes amazes me to see the world go out and put on a concert of some sort that is done in par excellence and captivates everyone's attention fully. However, the church will go out and shabbily throw something together with only one working speaker full of distortion and static, and say, "Wow, didn't we have a time tonight?" It was actually a wasted time, and the bottom line is that no souls were saved that day, and even if it were one or two, it could have been much more had the program been better prepared in a spirit of excellence. Remember, ministry costs money, especially if you operate in the spirit of excellence. As an obedient "Go ye..." believer, you must take the time to make an investment in the right sound equipment that you set up for such a program. This directly reflects one's main purpose and presentation of the kingdom of God. Not having sufficient speakers for such an event is equivalent to not having any speakers at all.

If your setup is in a relatively small area of no more than 3 to 5 acres, then maybe two speakers are sufficient; however, if the area is a lot larger, then perhaps three to five speakers might be more sufficient for your purpose. If the event you are organizing is large enough for an auditorium or a stadium crowd, then it would undoubtedly be to your advantage to get assistance from a professional sound technician for the proper setup to enhance your program or presentation properly.

5. Use other helpful tools for optimum results in your "Go ye..." endeavor. The Massive Outreach Approach centers on the spiritual needs of the masses as a whole. Therefore every effort should support your cause to win them to Christ's kingdom. Other tools could include a **stage setup** so your audience won't be restricted to viewing the backs of other people's heads, and also bring an ample amount of **chairs** for your audience to sit during the duration of your program. This makes it extremely convenient for them to relax as they are being ministered to. You could also use **fancy lighting** on your stage setup to enhance the performance of a live band or praise dancers. This would definitely work really well if your order of events consists of a short skit or even a full-length play. Helpful tools also include a **strong generator** with a sufficient amount of amperage to power up everything for this massive event, without having to borrow or pay for electricity from the nearest business—that is, if there is a business or facility nearby.

What Locations Are Good for Massive Evangelism?

Here is a list of places to target when starting an effective outreach to win the masses for the kingdom of God:

Community Centers. Passing out flyers in the immediate area of a community center would be most helpful. This way the neighborhood would be abreast and more apt to show up at the neighborhood community center for your program or ministry.

Orphanages. Preparing a children's program would be appropriate. Include things like comedy, toy giveaways, games and magic tricks.

Housing projects or apartment complexes. An adequate sound system is a must for such an endeavor. However, you must get permission from the resident manager well enough in advance to minimize any problems or misunderstandings that could occur.

Foreign missions in third-world countries. Planning ahead of time is crucial if you want favorable results. Also, fundraising events could make your goal more attainable for your entire group. The larger the number of your team, the more ground your group could cover in third-world countries. The gospel of Jesus is so desperately needed overseas and in third-world countries; the people are praying and waiting for someone to lend them a hand in helping to change their world. Remember, you and I are the only Jesus this world of ours will ever see!

Street corners or vacant parcels of land. Set up a PA system or megaphone and simply preach! If you have the boldness, just play dumb and do it until someone stops you—if anyone stops you at all.

Shelters. Homeless shelters and battered women's shelters are a must. These facilities survive by the compassion, investments, and monetary donations of charitable groups such as nonprofit organizations, churches, and volunteers. If your church or group can afford it, then bringing food to these facilities when you visit will give you a better chance of being invited back on a regular basis.

Prisons. Your church or group must attend a seminar to go through the proper certification to be cleared through your state. Simply call or visit your local prison chaplain for the specific protocol.

Mall parking lots. This is usually ideal for a more organized program or setup. You must get permission from the mall's administrative office well in advance for such a major undertaking. Each mall usually has its own set of rules.

Hospitals. You can visit and pray for the sick only if the individual allows prayer or visitation, if not, then peacefully and respectfully walk away. Depending on the condition or prognosis of the patient, sometimes only close family members can visit, one or two at a time. Massive evangelism is seldom done in hospitals unless it is specifically a children's hospital. Talk with the floor supervisor.

Convalescent or nursing homes. These facilities openly welcome groups and churches because oftentimes family members and relatives forsake their loved ones, and the facility allows outsiders to come in primarily to comfort the elderly. This will be a golden opportunity to share the love of Christ with our senior citizens with hands-on interaction. Not only can your group sing and share Christ with them, but also one-on-one interaction could include washing their hair, clipping their toenails, reading the Bible to them, and even praying for them and with them. Remember, if you live to be in your golden years, you would welcome this opportunity with open arms and remember, *"Whatever a man sows, that he will also reap"* (Galatians 6:7, NKJV).

Colleges and universities. If your group can partner with a religious group already a part of the college or university, then you should have permission to set up a program on campus, either outside in the open air or inside an auditorium. This could be an excellent opportunity to win as many people as possible on the campus to Christ.

Parks and local recreation centers. This usually requires a permit from your city or county Parks and Recreation Office. In most cases, a minimal deposit is required and refunded if the park remains in its original shape after your Outreach Program concludes. When granted, this could be one of your most auspicious moments to minister to the masses from all walks of life. You would have success with the one-on-one approach as well as speaking to the masses by way of a PA system. You just can't go wrong with this connection if this request is granted by your local Parks and Recreation Office.

Night Fishing

Jesus called us to be fishers of men, so as fishers of men, for the best results, we not only fish during the day time, but also at night or really early in the wee hours of the morning. The mistake most churches make in the body of Christ worldwide is that they always do what is convenient to the local church based on the schedules of the congregation. However, we are not on the church's time clock, but rather on the unsaved world's time clock. Most crimes such as rape, murder, home invasions, break-ins, and drunk-driving accidents take place during the evening or early morning hours. Also, much of the major corruptive activities that you hear about on the news usually occur during the night hours as well, including occult practices. There is an untapped arena of ministry at nighttime and during these early hours of the morning in places that are used as the Devil's playground. These locations include street corners where prostitutes hang out, night clubs, strip clubs, pubs, escort services, and gay and lesbian bars. When Jesus commanded us to "Go ye," did He specify daytime or nighttime? I really don't think the time of day had anything to do with it. He just meant for us to *go*!

In 2003, my wife, Betty, and I went to Los Angeles for our annual vacation. Among other stops we made, we visited the Dream Center Church pastored by Matthew Barnett, the son of Evangelist and Pastor Tommy Barnett. The church building itself holds true historic value and meaning. It is Angelus Temple, the original church founded, built, and pastored by Aimee Semple McPherson, one of the Lord's true generals. Needless to say, Betty and I were anxious to visit and to be a part of the service that Sunday. Right before service ended, Pastor Matthew made an important announcement. "All of those interested in being a part of the witnessing team that will minister to the prostitutes tonight, please show up in the church parking lot at midnight."

I thought, *Am I hearing right, did he say prostitutes? Did he say midnight?* Now just ask yourself, what church do you honestly know that has an evangelism program that goes out at *midnight* to start the ministry? This is indeed rare, so my wife and I signed up right away.

We showed up at eleven thirty, half an hour early for this excursion. We were extremely shocked to see that we were not the only ones, but there must have been between forty and sixty others who were fired up and ready to go as well. As it turned out, the minister over the prostitute ministry was unable to be there that night; however, the pastor in charge of the gay and lesbian ministry was present, so everyone loaded up on about five or six vans to head out to Sunset Boulevard in Hollywood. The Dream Center is an evangelistic church with more than 125 active ministries within the church itself. This group of forty to sixty people ministered from midnight until about four thirty in the morning. We must have covered about twelve or more gay and lesbian clubs within a fifteen- or twenty-mile stretch. My wife and I personally led over seventeen gays and lesbians to the Lord that night.

Even in the midst of our witnessing to the unsaved right on the Devil's turf in the Devil's den, God's word still convicted the hearts of those seventeen people my wife and I ministered to. I learned that morning when we were loading up the vans to return to the church that a total of about sixty-nine souls were saved and repented from sin in the midst of the gay and lesbian clubs that very early morning. Wow, to God be the glory! More churches should practice night fishing for souls for favorable results. Sure there is much danger; however, there is danger during the day hours as well. Either way, we must pray for the Lord's protection and leading regardless. Obeying the voice of the Lord this way is the Devil's absolute worst nightmare!

Message

Let's remember our acronym **AMP: Approach, Message, and Persuasion.** We've covered in detail our approach and how to make it work sufficiently with impressive results, now let's concentrate on the message we must deliver. There are no two people exactly alike, so having said that, everyone who answers the command of God to "Go ye..." must deliver the message of Jesus to the individual(s) to whom you are speaking in a way that is most comfortable to you. However, that way should not by any means deviate from or compromise the original message included in the Gospels. If the message is compromised or deviates in any way, shape, or form, then its meaning is totally different and your message has completely lost its efficacy and the saving power by which a soul is converted. Paul the apostle said in Romans 1:16, *"For I am not ashamed of the gospel of Christ: for it is the power of God unto salvation to every one that believeth; to the Jew first, and also to the Greek."* Notice that the gospel message is the *power of God unto salvation.* The Holy Spirit can only convict unsaved souls of sin if the gospel message of the cross, the power of God, has been conveyed properly.

The word *gospel* means "good news," therefore our message

should consist of hope, divine healing, prosperity, deliverance, destiny, purpose, forgiveness, eternal life, and compassion. All of this is good news, not negative, depressive, or even hopeless news. The world is used to hearing hopeless news on a daily basis anyway. The message should be made very simple and clear. You are simply trying to convey the love of God to the person you are witnessing to or ministering to by introducing Jesus Christ to him in a way that becomes a no-brainer. He must understand that he is a sinner (Romans 3:23) and that Jesus is the only one who can redeem and restore him to right standing with God the Father from the curse of sin, because *the wages of sin is death* (Romans 6:23). Let him know that God accepts him just the way he is, no matter how terrible a person he feels he may be or that you might feel he is. However, when one accepts Him into his life, He'll begin a process of deliverance inside of that individual. **In the message of Christ you are conveying, you may want to allude to His miraculous birth, His life, His death on the cross, His burial, His resurrection, His ascension, and His soon return.**

Under no circumstances are you ever to condemn the person or people with whom you are sharing Christ, no matter how bad they might seem. You and I are no better than the people with whom we share the good news. The only difference is that we were once that person ourselves, and presently are perpetually working on our own salvation humbly and consistently. Without the help of the Holy Spirit, we all would be doomed for an eternal hell. So with this in mind, put yourself in that person's position, and let the love of Jesus manifest itself through your example. Please keep in mind that you and I are the only Jesus the world will ever see! Look at it this way: Condemnation is a tool used by the Devil to remind people of how unworthy they are and how doomed eternally they may be; however, conviction is used by the Holy Spirit to allow the individual to want to make a change for the better in life by choosing Christ. Now which would you prefer to use—condemnation or conviction?

When it comes to speaking to more than one individual at a time, such as a small group or even a massive amount of people at once, then by all means keep your message as short and simple as possible. It is one thing to preach to an entire congregation on a given Sunday or midweek service, but it is an entirely different thing to minister to crowds of unsaved people who have made their way out to be present in church while Satan fought them every step of the way. Christians come to church with the intent of getting fed the Word of God with expectancy in their hearts. However, the unsaved come out for the baits or attractions, the singing, curiosity, or because someone is constantly twisting their arms to come, or possibly because they felt in their hearts a tug of the Holy Spirit and a need to change and gravitate toward the things of God. So with this in mind, if your message is too long and you sound too preachy, as if you're preaching to a regular church crowd on Sundays, then you'll probably lose your audience. The message for the unsaved is to be prepared differently than for the saved audience. The emphasis of the message should be on their desperate need for Christ and His forgiving power, so that during an altar call they can respond in the proper way with genuine repentance in their hearts through conviction of the Holy Spirit. Try to limit your entire message to about thirty minutes or less. **It is not about the length of your message, but it is totally about the strength of your message.** Keep to about thirty minutes or less as a general rule, unless there is a divine intervention of the Holy Spirit that comes in and moves and shakes the place in an awesome way. At that point, the Holy Spirit is in complete control and one must totally yield to His leading.

Understand that you are literally speaking as the very mouthpiece of the Lord God Almighty at this point, and that all of heaven is backing you up when you open your mouth with boldness to the people as you speak to them with love. While Satan in the spirit realm is fighting them with doubt, confusion, hindrance, and apathy, Almighty God and His angels are on your side backing up every word that comes from your mouth. Isaiah 55:11 says, *"So shall my word be that goeth forth out of my mouth: it shall not return unto me void, but it shall accomplish that which I please, and it shall prosper in the thing whereto I sent it."* Even if you are not called to be a preacher, just the mere fact that you are handling God's word as a "Go ye" believer qualifies you with spiritual backup and comfort, because at this juncture you are a carrier of God's word, and as Isaiah says, His word shall not return unto Him void. God means just that! As we are used as the mouthpiece of the Lord, it is His responsibly to bring about the conviction through the Holy Ghost into individual lives that will confess and receive the Father into their hearts.

Persuasion

Having them Pray the Prayer of Salvation

Now as fishers of men, we must bring them to the net and get ready to catch them into the kingdom of God, but the only way this can even be done is through convincing and strong **Persuasion by our message.** So far, the approaches used have gotten us this far, and without a doubt, the message of Christ's love has held their attention up to this point; now the deal must be sealed. The way we seal a deal is again through strong persuasion. Now, through persuasive means, comes the time we can finally introduce them to **the ABCs of Salvation: Admit, Believe, Confess.** After that, we lead them into the Prayer of Salvation.

Admit. They must absolutely admit that they do have sin in their lives. This is done through our message that we've shared with them, pretty much like a surgeon skillfully uses a surgical knife. The word of God shared with them cuts them to the core of their souls and spirit (Hebrews 4:12). How can one expect to be remotely forgiven of any such sin if there is no admittance of sin in their lives at all? Many people by nature feel in their hearts that they are fine. Others feel a sense of apathy and use the fact that "we're all human" as a common excuse to continue sinning as if it's no big deal. They shrug it off as if to say, "Who are you to tell me about sin? We're all sinners." Sometimes pride and arrogance keeps them from admitting that they have failed and that they do need help apart from themselves. As long as humans feel that everything is together in their lives, then they really don't feel a strong need to admit that they are living their lives totally contrary to the will of God. But when people come to the end of themselves to the degree that they know their actions thus far are a complete failure, that is the point where the Holy Spirit can come in and take control of a person's life. The Bible teaches us that *godly sorrow produces repentance unto salvation* (2 Corinthians 7:10). When we come to the end of ourselves in weakness or are at our wit's end, we need a Savior to throw out a lifeline in order for us to stay afloat. It is at this point that Jesus is willing to step in and show Himself strong in us through the admittance of our sins and unworthiness. This is the job of the Christian to convey this message to the individual without sounding self-righteous or pious, but humble and compassionate, for if it had not been for the Lord Jesus forgiving us, we ourselves would be lost and without a Savior in our lives. **As a rule of thumb remember, if we admit it, then we are empowered to quit it.**

Believe. One must be convinced and believe in his heart that Jesus is indeed the Son of the living God. The Bible teaches us that *without faith, it is impossible to please Him: for he that cometh to God must believe that He is, and that He is a rewarder of them that diligently seek Him* (Hebrews 11:6). As the Christian soul winner, you must persuade your person of assignment that he must believe and accept the fact the Jesus Christ is indeed the Son of the living God. He came down from heaven in flesh form and paid the price for the sin of the whole world by dying on behalf of every person on the planet. If a person is not at the point of believing that Jesus is Lord and Savior and that he died for the sin of the world, then that person is simply not ready, so don't waste precious time on him at this point. However, put him on your prayer list so the Lord will not allow judgment upon him, and so His word that has been sown in that individuals heart will not return unto Him void. If you are successful in convincing the person to believe that Jesus is Lord and Savior, then lead him to the very next step.

Confess. One definition of the word confess is **"to acknowledge one's belief or faith in; declare adherence to."** The Bible says in Romans 10:9–10 (AB) *"Because if you acknowledge and confess with your lips that Jesus is Lord and in your heart believed (adhere to, trust in, and rely on the truth) that God raised Him from the dead, you will be saved. For with the heart a person believes (adheres to, trusts in, and relies on Christ) and so is justified (declared righteous, acceptable to God), and with the mouth he confesses (declares openly and speaks out freely his faith) and confirms (his) salvation."* Confession that Jesus is Lord is to say that Satan is no longer lord over one's life, instead, Jesus Christ is by way of one's confession. This final step seals the entire deal of leading an individual to Christ.

Prayer of Salvation

This simple prayer of salvation will break the lordship of Satan over a person's life and establish the Lordship of Jesus Christ. The key to this prayer is for the person praying it not to merely repeat words, but to mean them earnestly from his heart as he prays. This prayer is not the only prayer to pray in order to lead an individual, but this is the way the Lord leads me to lead others, so feel free to use this one as a model, or tweak it to your liking.

> *"Father God, I admit that I'm a sinner and that I have sinned against you, Lord. I humbly ask that Jesus Christ come into my heart as my personal Lord and Savior. I believe that you died for my sins on the cross and that God raised you up from the dead on the third day. So I ask that you please forgive me for all my sins that I've committed, and that you wash me clean by your precious blood. Now I sincerely confess you as my Lord and Savior. Keep me from the evil one, Satan, and let your Holy Spirit constantly strengthen me daily in areas of weakness in my life. Help me, Father, to be strong so the destiny you have for my life will be fulfilled in me, in Jesus' name, Amen!*

Follow-Up: Discipleship

Congratulations, you did it! You are now responsible for leading someone to the Lord Jesus. You are indeed an ambassador of Christ. There is absolutely no feeling of ecstasy that can be compared to the feeling of singlehandedly snatching a soul out of the dark clutches of Satan's kingdom, and delivering him as a new creature into the kingdom of our Lord Jesus. Hallelujah, hallelujah! Now let's review the Great Commission in its entirety:

"Go ye therefore, and teach all nations, baptizing them in the name of the Father, and of the Son, and of the Holy Ghost: Teaching them to observe all things whatsoever I have commanded you: and, lo, I am with you always, even unto the end of the world. Amen." (Matthew 28:19–20)

The command "Go ye" is first given. Well, you've successfully done this, now what? Notice the end of the verse and the second part where it says, "baptizing them in the name of the Father, and of the Son, and of the Holy Ghost: Teaching them to observe all things whatsoever I have commanded you." This deals with the topic of **Follow-Up!**

Remember **our primary goal is threefold: win them, teach and train them (discipleship), and then send them out to win others.**

There is a lot more to it than just going out to all nations. Other responsibilities include baptizing them and teaching them. All of this is where follow-up occurs. What exactly is follow-up? It's making sure that the new believer is well grounded in the kingdom of God so he will be trained in the teachings of Christ to the degree that he will be strong and mature enough to stand on his own and make other disciples in time.

God has commissioned each one of us as an evangelist; however, the entire threefold ministry comes into play when we follow up with that new convert. After we've caught the fish, we must now begin to clean it and prepare it. That new convert must now be established and planted in a local church so he is taught the word of God by that local pastor. It is very important that you make sure **the right pastor is chosen for the right job.** The pastor whom God has established has the responsibility of feeding the flock fresh manna from heaven every week. The new convert should be handled like a newborn baby, because to the new convert, this is all new no matter what physical age he may be. He must be fed the sincere milk of the word of God (1 Peter 2:2). Again, this training is for the growth and maturity of the new believer until he is spiritually able to stand on his very own. Even then, at that point he duplicates the process of **"each one reach one."** Follow-up is so important that without it, every effort put into play would eventually be nullified and put to naught. God holds the entire body of Christ in contempt if follow-up is not instituted in our "Go ye" plan.

The order of God is for us to *"Go ye therefore into all the world and preach the gospel unto every creature,* (**win them,** so they'll know who Christ is and accept Him), *baptizing them in the name of the Father, and of the Son, and of the Holy Ghost: Teaching them to observe all things whatsoever I have commanded you* (**teach and train them** through baptism and discipleship), *lo, I am with you always, even unto the end of the world."* **Send them;** as we go, Jesus is with us.

Telephone Follow-up

As each new convert approaches the altar during the altar call of a church service, please see to it that someone writes down the convert's name, address, phone number, and e-mail address. Following up with a phone call or an e-mail within two or three days will also reassure the new convert of his importance and relevance in the eyes of our heavenly Father as well as your local church. This not only makes him feel very important, but also acts as a shield in his life as he faces the reality of being tempted by Satan to return to his previous situation, which may need direct and serious attention. A telephone follow-up ministry is seriously needed in all churches that have an evangelism program. This ministry could literally save the lives of individuals who may have completely given up on life. This is a very timely ministry that could even save someone from suicide.

Establish a Foundations in Christianity Class for New Converts

A teaching class should be established in every church that does in fact have an evangelism program. This class should consist of twelve to twenty-six weeks of new-convert training, ending with a test to measure the students' ability and progress. These classes should be set up in a way that limits the new convert's active participation in ministry until proper training is complete and the test passed.

Immediately after the altar call, when souls come forth to surrender their hearts unto the Lord, there should be a room set up for them to get further instructions so they won't get lost in the shuffle of the church routine. Materials should be passed out that help the new convert become familiar with the ministries that exist in your church, along with an appeal for them to attend your Foundations In Christianity New Converts Classes.

Proper follow-up teaching will include the following list of precepts to ensure the new believer of proper and healthy growth in the Lord:

1. **Assurance of their salvation** *(1 John 5:13, Ephesians 2:8–9)*
2. **Their Identity in Christ** *(Psalm 139:13–16, Peter 2:9, Ephesians 2:6, Jeremiah 29:11, Ephesians 1:4–5, Ephesians 2:10, Psalm 139:1–4, Colossians 2:13–14, John 1:12–13, Galatians 4:6–7, 1 Samuel 16:7, John 15:15, Romans 5:1–2, Colossians 3:12, Galatians 3:26–27, Psalm 138:8, 1 Thessalonians 1:4–6, Romans 8:14–15, Colossians 3:3–4, Ephesians 2:19, 1 Thessalonians 5:5, Philippians 3:20, Hebrews 3:14, Matthew 5:13, 2 Corinthians 1:21–22, 1 John 3:1, Matthew 5:14, 1 Corinthians 3:16, Romans 6:18, 1 John 5:18, 2 Corinthians 5:17–21, 1 Peter 2:5)*
3. **Their need to know that man is a tripartite being, spirit, soul, and body** *(1 Thessalonians 5:23)*
4. **Importance of daily devotion, consisting of prayer and Bible study** *(2 Timothy 2:15, John 5:39, Luke 18:1, Ephesians 6:18)*
5. **Knowing the weapons of our warfare** *(2 Corinthians 10:4–5)*

6. The importance of relying on the Holy Spirit for all our needs *(Acts 9:31, Romans 8:26, Acts 1:8, Acts 2:1–4, John 14:17, John 14:26, John 15:26, John 16:13–14, Ephesians 4:30, 2 Corinthians 14:6, Matthew 3:16)*

7. Watching out for the wicked evil one Satan and being aware of his tactics *(Matthew 13:19, 2 Corinthian 2:11, Matthew 7:15, 2 Corinthians 11:14)*

8. Beware of the works of the flesh and avoid them *(Galatians 5:19–21)*

9. Knowing the nine fruits of the Spirit that should operate in us *(Galatians 5:22–23)*

10. Operating in the gifts of the Spirit *(1 Corinthians 12:7–11)*

11. Knowing our authority as believers in Christ *(Ephesians 1:17–23, Luke 10:19–20, Ephesians 2:6, Isaiah 54:17, 2 Corinthians 10:3–5)*

12. The importance of tithes and offerings *(Malachi 3:8–12, 2 Corinthians 9:6–8)*

13. Sharing their Christian faith with others as they become a "Go ye" believer *(Matthew 28:19–20, Ezekiel 3:18-2, 2 Corinthians 5:17–20, Acts 1:8)*

Other teachings could include...
- The importance of baptism
- The importance of church attendance
- The meaning of fasting and its benefits
- The divisions of the Bible-Old and New Testaments
- The different avenues in which God speaks to us
- The will of God
- The seven Hebrew ways of worship
- The wisdom of the Lord
- The ways of God

Child of God, Let's "Go ye" into all the world for the Lord, and knock the Devil completely out of commission by snatching souls out of darkness into the kingdom of light in the Lord!

I have for years had on my home office desk a plaque that simply reads, **"Only one life, 'twill soon be past. Only what's done for Christ will last."** That phrase pretty much sums up the Christian life to me. My sincere desire for you is that you take inventory of your life daily, and ask yourself one simple question: "Have I pleased the Lord in the personal affairs of my life today?" My desire is to please my heavenly Father wholeheartedly. I so desperately want to leave my mark on this earth and give the Devil a black eye he'll never forget. **My hope is that when the Devil has nightmares, you and I are the Christians whose faces he sees!**

Life is too short, so go out all the way for Jesus and win as many souls for Christ as you possibly can! And remember, not only will many people have to thank you when you get to heaven, but also let's not forget the Lord's benefits because they are literally **out of this world!**

THE END!

CPSIA information can be obtained at www.ICGtesting.com
Printed in the USA
LVOW080055050613

336905LV00001B/3/P